What makes a Champion!

Over fifty extraordinary individuals share their insights

Editor

Allan Snyder

 World Scientific

NEW JERSEY · LONDON · SINGAPORE · BEIJING · SHANGHAI · HONG KONG · TAIPEI · CHENNAI

Published by

World Scientific Publishing Co. Pte. Ltd.

5 Toh Tuck Link, Singapore 596224

USA office: 27 Warren Street, Suite 401-402, Hackensack, NJ 07601

UK office: 57 Shelton Street, Covent Garden, London WC2H 9HE

Library of Congress Cataloging-in-Publication Data
What makes a champion! : over fifty extraordinary individuals share their insights / edited by
Allan Snyder.
   pages cm
  Reprint, originally published in 2002 by Penguin Books.
  Includes bibliographical references.
  ISBN-13 978-9814612845 (alk. paper) -- ISBN-10 9814612847 (alk. paper)
  1. Success--Psychological aspects. 2. Self-actualization (Psychology) I. Snyder, Allan.
  BF637.S8W4165 2014
  158.1--dc23

                    2014016583

British Library Cataloguing-in-Publication Data
A catalogue record for this book is available from the British Library.

Design adapted from the original Penguin Books edition, by Karen Trump, Penguin Design Studio.

In-house Editor: Juliet Lee Ley Chin

Printed in Singapore

To Gavin Brown
Visionary Leader — Academic Champion

ABOUT THE EDITOR

Dr Allan Snyder is recognised for groundbreaking discoveries covering the fields of visual neurobiology, communications, optical physics, and the mind sciences. He received the world's "foremost prize in communication and information technology", the Marconi International Prize, in New York City. He is a Fellow of the Royal Society of London and the recipient of its 2001 Clifford Paterson Prize for "contributions which benefit mankind".

A graduate of Harvard University, MIT, and University College London, he was also a Guggenheim Fellow at Yale University's School of Medicine and a Royal Society Research Fellow at the Physiology Laboratories of Cambridge University.

His scientific discoveries are the subject of documentaries and media attention worldwide. The New York Times declared his hypothesis that everyone possesses the extraordinary skills of savants, "a breakthrough that could lead to a revolution in the way we understand ... the functioning of the human brain".

The Creator of What Makes a Champion?™, designated an official Olympic Cultural Event for Sydney 2000 and Beijing 2008, Dr Snyder founded the Centre for the Mind and co-founded Emotiv — the pioneering brain-computer interface company. He was singled out at the 2010 Shanghai Expo as a "Master of Innovation" for the idea that launched Emotiv. In 2012 he was voted among the 10 Most Creative People in Higher Education. Further information may be found at www.centreforthemind.com.

FOREWORD

What Makes a Future Champion?

'What makes a champion — and I mean a champion in the broadest sense of the word — is the champion mindset... The champion mindset is the transferable commodity and not the skill itself'. This is the key insight which we find in Professor Snyder's remarkable celebration of individual achievement: *What Makes a Champion!*

The elegant simplicity of Professor Snyder's theory of champion mindset belies the profound nature of his discovery. You hold in your hand a distillation of the three key elements of championship — a blueprint for understanding what separates the true champions from the rest of humanity. This is not some impenetrable academic treatise, blinding the reader with science and complex analysis. These are the real-life stories of great achievers, told with a first-hand immediacy — stories which illustrate 'the fundamental aspect of mind' that enables the champion to achieve extraordinary success; a mindset that drives the special few to 'challenge others and to expand our horizons'.

Allan Snyder is a visionary thinker, and, as an organisation, we were drawn to that vision over a decade ago. From its beginnings in Sydney, Australia in 1998, MindChamps' educational philosophy was always to find, within each individual, the unique qualities which could be tapped to turn that person into a champion learner for life.*

This is why the research of Professor Snyder and the Centre for the Mind struck such a resonant chord with us. Working with young people, we recognised that the champion mindset offered the crucial ingredient for empowering them for future achievement. Over the intervening years, our collaboration with Professor Snyder has allowed us to bring the fruits of his revolutionary discovery to thousands of young people, and for this we are eternally grateful.

What Makes a Champion! is the perfect handbook for identifying — and inculcating — a winning attitude in all people, young and not so young — which is why this book forms a key part of our programs for all our students and their parents.

David Chiem
Founder and Chairman
MindChamps Holdings Pte Limited
April 2014

---

*Further information about MindChamps can be found at: www.mindchamps.org.

PREFACE TO THE REPRINT EDITION OF *WHAT MAKES A CHAMPION!*

Few things are more compelling than knowing what makes a champion. Answering this has been my long-term objective. It motivated the original Penguin publication *What Makes a Champion!*[1], *where* over 50 extraordinary individuals advance their insight on the question. Since that original publication, many have come forward to support my thesis[2,3,4] that what makes a champion is a *champion mindset*. This mindset conveys the courage to challenge others and to expand our horizons. Its cardinal manifestation is a person's propensity to pour something that is uniquely them into whatever they do. Champions abhor being just one of the pack! Programs[5] now exist to instil the champion mindset, especially in children, at a time when it is imbued most effectively.

This reprint edition allows a new audience access to the wisdom of extraordinary achievers — real champions in the broadest sense of the word.

Professor Emeritus Allan Snyder
Chairman, What Makes a Champion?
Founder, Centre for the Mind
University of Sydney, April 2014

1. A. Snyder, *What Makes a Champion!*, Penguin, 2002.
2. A. Snyder, The Inaugural Edwin Flack Lecture, Australian Olympic Committee, Sydney 26 June 1998.
3. A. Snyder, International Olympic Review, XXVI–VII, June–July, pp. 71–74 (1999).
4. A. Snyder, Their Winning Ways, *The Australian*, 8–9 April 2000.
5. Programs for pre-school to tertiary level by international award-winning education institute MindChamps, headquartered in Singapore.

CONTENTS

INTRODUCTION

I am captivated by extraordinary success. I have always wanted to know what makes a champion – and I mean a champion in the broadest sense of the word. I see championship as a fundamental aspect of the mind, the aspect responsible for advancing civilisation. Furthermore, I believe that everyone is a potential champion. So we should all be compelled to understand the factors that nurture and amplify extraordinary achievement.

Imagine the competitive advantage for those who possess such knowledge. Understanding championship is a valuable product. It is ultimately the greatest product of all, because the great nations of the future will be those that can export the products of their minds. The more we understand our innate potential to be champions, the better.

Propelled by this motivation, the Centre for the Mind conceived the 'What Makes a Champion?' event on the eve of the 2000 Olympics at the Great Hall of the University of Sydney. Here, Nelson Mandela led a cast of timeless champions to synergise in the common goal of unravelling the universals of great success. This book offers their views alongside those of other extraordinary individuals who were unable to attend the occasion.

We envisaged the 2000 Sydney Olympics as both the opportune moment and the quintessential venue for the exploration of human achievement. But not achievement limited only to sports; rather, human achievement across the board, across the spectrum.

Of course, sport itself gives insights into the universals of championship.

If you think about it, athletes might be considered neurotic. Coaches have often made that call. How else can you explain why a person, for a mere abstraction, would actually drive himself to physical collapse? How else can you explain the single-minded dedication of an Olympic champion?

But is there really any difference between the so-called neurosis of the athlete and that of the artist, the scientist, or for that matter any individual who commits herself to realise a dream? In all cases there is a sacrifice of the pleasures in life as normally appreciated.

What elusive spirit sustains champions through the agonising process necessary to achieve greatness, necessary to realise a dream? If we answer this question we will have unlocked one of the mysteries of the mind. We will have discovered the element common to all great achievers. If we answer this question we will have captured the crucial ingredient that lets the human spirit soar.

Ultimately I believe that what makes a champion is a champion mindset. The champion mindset, not the skill itself, is the transferable commodity. If you have done something great in one field, you are far more likely to do so in another.

It is our mindsets that limit our expectations of ourselves and circumscribe our boundaries. It is our mindsets that determine whether we have the courage to challenge others and to expand our horizons.

The celebrated Sigmund Freud aptly captured this sentiment when he said: 'I am not really a man of science, not an observer, not an experimenter and not a thinker. I am nothing but . . . an adventurer . . . a conquistador with the boldness and the tenacity of that type of being.'

How can we identify the champion mindset and how can it be nurtured? Our research gives us some clues.

Champions often have an aversion to being average – they want to be not necessarily better than others, just not like the rest. This quality frequently appears early in life in the form of a stoic independence, rebellion or unconventional tastes.

Champions are often familiar with adversity. They have had to 'fight' to get where they are and they continue to do so at some level, say by ignoring the body's warning signals, by denying themselves normal pleasures, or by setting challenges that seem unreachable. Many champions have severe disabilities – such as Churchill's bouts of 'black dog' depression, Roosevelt's crippling polio, Darwin's daily vomiting attacks and the legion of athletes who triumph despite their struggles with asthma.

Champions often fail, but that doesn't discourage them in the long haul. They learn how to convert, as McKinsey's Michael Rennie says, 'upsets into set-ups' for something better. Abraham Lincoln lost over and over again before stage-managing his sensational election as President.

Many of the world's greatest scientists were at best average students. Things just didn't come easily. At the other extreme, child prodigies rarely rise to the top of their profession – and they are by definition the ones who found learning effortless.

Those who learn effortlessly in youth may well be at a disadvantage in tackling seemingly unsurmountable problems. Struggling in the early learning process possibly acclimatises us to difficulties, and may advantage us in dealing with adversity because we then see difficulties as being a matter of course.

Surprisingly, what emerged from our research is the possible necessity of overcoming adversity as a preparation for being a champion, even adversity created by oneself, say in setting goals beyond reach.

Sir Edmund Hillary is especially eloquent on this subject. 'You must always set another challenge.' At the top of Everest he was mentally planning the ascent of the next mountain. 'Go for something outrageous . . . challenge

MICHAEL L'ESTRANGE
Australia's High Commissioner to London
(formerly Federal Cabinet Secretary)

AUSTRALIA IS A NATION OF THE twenty-first century – technologically sophisticated, culturally diverse, adaptable, questing, innovative and optimistic. Allan Snyder's brainchild What Makes a Champion? sought to capture these dimensions of Australia, and did so dramatically well.

One of the distinctive achievements of What Makes a Champion? lay not only in its reflective analysis of what has set the champions of the past apart from their rivals but also in the pointers it gave for the champions of the future to realise their potential.

But perhaps more than anything else, What Makes a Champion? reflected the diversity of modern Australia. It highlighted that, whether it be in matters of the mind or the fields of sporting endeavour, Australians bring a unique perspective, a special focus and a capacity for surprise.

What Makes a Champion? was an important event for Australia but had implications for people everywhere. The fact that it took place in Sydney during that unforgettable Olympic period says much about the true dimensions of modern Australia, the real scope of the Olympic movement and the commitment to excellence on the part of all who conceived and participated in it.

yourself' – create adversity. 'If you know you can do it, don't do it,' says Hillary. 'You might as well go to the beach.'

Magistrate Pat O'Shane drew strength from overcoming adversity imposed upon her by society: 'It is no good to have an easy life'; and marathon swimmer Shelley Taylor-Smith derived strength from the acute pain of jellyfish stings.

We can learn from this that it is crucial to continually reach for the stars by setting challenges that extend us and, by necessity, require us to overcome adversity.

We especially need to anticipate adversity and look upon it as both a challenge and a learning experience. But this aspect of our findings is more profound than merely engaging in positive thinking. It is integral to a champion mindset. And it requires a fundamental shift in our relationship with adversity, especially for parents whose children are having difficulty.

Champions have the courage to break rules. Obviously, to be a champion it is crucial to know the foundations of the discipline, whether it is the mathematical structure of physics, the rules for serving a hamburger or the appropriate routines for athletic training.

But champions seem to differentiate themselves from others with equivalent training by having the courage to experiment with the rules and to invent new ways of doing things. Even in sports, it takes courage to break with a conventional training regime.

Peter Ritchie, Non-Executive Chairman of McDonald's, tells how over the years he has taken kids off the street and trained them in the basic elementary rules of serving hamburgers. And he says that from this training procedure a number of great leaders of McDonald's have emerged both here and abroad.

But then I asked how the great leaders at McDonald's are identified from a group required only to learn simple rules. Easy, Peter said: they are the ones who break the rules.

I believe that this example serves as a metaphor for success. Anyone can learn the rules of physics. They just take longer to learn than those for serving hamburgers. But the great physicist is the one who invents new ways to look at things. Einstein was not an especially brilliant student. His brilliance emerged later, not when he was learning the rules of physics but when he was questioning the conventional wisdom of his discipline.

Much of our research has shown that champions execute their skill unconsciously. Their actions and decisions are often intuitive and not based on conscious logic. This is in contrast to the process of learning itself, which is logical, and a comparative struggle. Yet in our society trusting intuition is often condemned.

For example, when CEOs are under threat they often adopt conservative strategies instead of taking bold risks as they usually would. Yet it was their successful risk-taking that got them to the top in the first place. Adopting the conservative, logical strategy is the antithesis of what makes them a champion. Champions learn to trust their intuition, especially when threatened.

In this book you will meet champions from all walks of life, people whose outlooks, ideologies and experiences are vastly different. But they all have in common being winners at what they do. They are champions in their field. Each conveys a highly personal and unique perspective on what makes a champion.

There's someone in this book who will reach out to you. There's someone in this book who will inspire you.

Nelson Mandela says it is easier to change society than it is to change yourself. John Eales salutes his parents for their unconditional love. Poppy King reflects on being 'persona non grata', and former Philippines President Corazon Aquino speaks of the strength she drew from her supporters' faith in her and from her own religious belief. Ralph Doubell's description of his gold medal win at the Rome Olympic Games is a gripping portrayal of the adversities that can strike even at the threshold of triumph.

The messages are profound and will work on you unconsciously to build a champion mindset. Ultimately, I believe, they amplify the championship potential in us all.

Inevitably, I am asked to single out my champions. So I do just that on pages 211–213.

My colleagues and I delight in this journey to understand what makes a champion, and to establish a permanent intellectual component to the Olympic movement modelled on our Sydney 2000 event.

Allan Snyder

ACKNOWLEDGEMENTS

A project of this magnitude does not materialise from thin air. It takes an army of supporters, totally committed individuals with supreme talent, all of whom share a common vision, all of whom are passionate about ensuring its reality.

Prime Minister Mr John Howard grasped the significance of the What Makes a Champion? project from my first visit to his office in early 1998. He, along with the then Federal Cabinet Secretary, Michael L'Estrange, personally ensured much of our success.

A committee of superstars steered us through the inevitable difficulties we faced in the lead-up to the event on the eve of the Olympics.

I salute the dream team of Sean Barrett, CEO, Edelson; Gavin Brown, Vice-Chancellor, University of Sydney; Herb Elliott, Director of Corporate Affairs, Australian Olympic Committee; Jim Ferguson, Executive Director of the Australian Sports Commission; Alex Hamill, Chairman, The Communications Group; James Millar, Deputy CEO, Ernst & Young; and Karl Sergeant, Brand and Marketing Director, AMP.

Crucial insights were provided by our multidisciplinary research team including mediator Bradley Chenowith, biologist Dr Michael Djordjevic, sociologist Professor Janet George, behavioural strategist Andrew

Miekle, international relations specialist Roland Rich, sports psychologist Justine Stynes, visual anthropologist Professor Michael Vischer and linguist Dr Michael Walsh.

The herculean task of inspiring intellectual depth plus exhilarating entertainment rested in the hands of several media celebrities: Maxine McKew, George Negus, Peter Thompson and Margaret Throsby.

My warmest appreciation goes to our intellectual partners, AMP, Ernst & Young and the University of Sydney, who worked with us at every stage of the project. All of our staff at the Centre for the Mind devoted a super-human effort, especially Megan Cusack, and Robyn Gerber (sponsored to us by Ernst & Young). And thank you to Stuart Stark, a brilliant editor, who assisted me at every turn in bringing the wisdom of these giants to everyone.

Finally, I proudly acknowledge that the Centre for the Mind (www.centreforthemind.com) is mentored by some of the best minds in the nation, including Phillip Adams, David Armstrong, Baz Luhrmann and Lachlan Murdoch. The Centre is a joint venture of Australia's two pre-eminent universities: Australia's first university, the University of Sydney, and Australia's national university, the Australian National University. Their support, along with that of our foundation sponsor, News Limited, catapulted the What Makes a Champion? project into reality.

Allan Snyder

WHAT MAKES A CHAMPION?

A champion is someone who makes a difference. These people are everywhere ... It is the people crazy enough to believe they can change the world who actually do.

Poppy King

I'm sure there is a champion mindset. I can perhaps describe it as a mindset that blocks out all else apart from the goal or task at hand.

John Eales

Memorable champions ... rise above their achievements and make their mark on history by displaying exemplary human values.

Dr Ian Gawler

To serve the poor, to sing great songs, to do great research in the laboratory. Those things it seems to me are available to a multitude of people.

Richard Butler

We have power to influence people's lives. I think the ethical content becomes very important, maybe the most important thing.

Malcolm Fraser

It is easier to change the community in which we live. But what is more difficult is to change yourself.

Nelson Mandela

RICHARD BUTLER

Australian Ambassador for Disarmament to the United Nations, then Ambassador to the UN, then Executive Chair of the UN Special Commission charged with the disarmament of Iraq. He convened the Canberra Commission on the Elimination of Nuclear Weapons, which led to the UN adopting the Nuclear Test Ban Treaty. He arguably has a higher international profile than any other living Australian.

Butler says that belief in the goal, rather than the glory, sustains a champion.

HOW DO YOU DRAW THE DISTINCTION BETWEEN DETERMINATION to succeed and personal ambition? This question implies the existence of two aspects of human behaviour: determination and ambition. The question also asserts that a distinction can be drawn between these two motivations and, indeed, that this distinction is a crucial one.

The foundation for this assertion is the difference between motivation directed towards the achievement of an identified objective outside of the self; and the achievement of success, reward or recognition for the self.

An example of the first of these is when a person is motivated by bettering the time needed to be achieved to break a record in running or swimming, or by finding the solution to a problem in immunology. The second motivation occurs when the focus of the actor is rather more on the medal that is awarded and the personal accolade that follows the victory in the race or the laboratory. Many would argue that, in practical terms, this is a distinction without a difference, and therefore a useless and possibly negative one. Surely, it is argued, any person striving to achieve a goal is typically motivated by the belief in that goal and the wish to succeed. Divide these two sources of motivation, and the most likely outcome will be failure both to achieve the objective goal and to achieve the desired personal ambition or recognition.

What is at issue is the dynamic interaction between the human personality and will, and objective reality. It is possible to identify an optimal form of that interaction and a negative form.

A central aspect of objective reality (which will be faced by any person determined to achieve a goal and/or personal recognition or reward) will be obstacles and barriers, including those that appear impassable or terminal. The reaction of the individual actor to such challenges is the decisive determinant of his/her staying the course and finishing it. At its root, the choice is between stopping and conceding defeat or rejecting any such concession. The champion chooses the latter.

The ability to make that choice, to turn a disadvantage into an advantage, to make a positive out of what seems to be wholly negative, relies on two strengths: conviction about the rightness of the goal and the ability to divest oneself of the aspects of ego and self-aggrandisement. These two strengths, together, form positive determination.

> *The choice is between stopping and conceding defeat or rejecting any such concession. The champion chooses the latter.*

The second inner source of strength is more contentious, as it flies in the face of the popularised notion that personal ambition, the striving for personal reward and recognition, is a key motivator of success. Of course it is, but it alone does not make a champion.

If an actor views obstacles as threatening to themselves – rather than threatening to the goal – the reaction of such an actor will be distorted by the ego and result in a spectrum of choices. These choices range from giving up, at one end of the spectrum, to redefining the point of the game, moving the goalposts, declaring the game a waste of time, or even cheating, at the other end. These strategies may succeed, sometimes spectacularly, and can thus appear to be innovative. Eventually, however, they will fail because choices made for the wrong reasons cannot endure.

> *The greatest evils have been based on the substitution of personal ambition for objective good. When such ambition has been joined by inhuman ideas it has proven deadly.*

In this context, a key lesson from history, from the political sphere of human life, is that the greatest evils have been based on the substitution of personal ambition for objective good. When such ambition has been joined by inhuman ideas it has proven deadly.

However, stories of heroes in politics, research, the

arts or sport always emphasise their belief in the goal. That this point is self-evident does not empty it of its meaning. In fact, it has a deeper meaning.

I pose the existence of objective goods. The actor is the means to the end. When the powerful dynamic of human personality and will is directed to the achievement of such goods, they are likely to be achieved, precisely because of their objective value. This is the possibility hinted at in the saying 'necessity is the mother of invention'. This is the logic of goal-directed determination, not of self-aggrandisement. This possibility is available in every field of human endeavour, and on any scale.

One of the main sources of breakdown along this path is the substitution of the subjective role of the actor for the objective virtue of the goal. The stamp of the champion is their ability to make the distinction between subjective and objective good.

The source of that clear sight is inner balance. That balance is identified as essential by the ancient Greeks and taught by all of the great human wisdoms. If necessity is the mother of invention, then this balance is its father. Champions display this balance and show in their attitude towards their own success that the goal, rather than self-aggrandisement, motivated them.

The stamp of the champion is their ability to make the distinction between subjective and objective good.

Finally, the concept of the champion has two main definitions: the winner or titleholder, and the defender or advocate of a cause. By definition there can only be one of the former; but there are countless numbers of the latter, anonymously at work every day selflessly defending the oppressed, sick, dispossessed, and forgotten of our world. These workers make the crucial distinction between determination and ambition.

They are also champions.

MAGISTRATE PAT O'SHANE

Profoundly influential, she has been an active contributor to Australia's social discourse since the 1970s. She became the first Aboriginal barrister in 1976, and the first Aboriginal magistrate in the New South Wales courts. O'Shane has been an impassioned spokesperson on women's and indigenous issues for many years, and was recognised in 1998 as one of Australia's National Living Treasures.

She says being a champion should ultimately benefit the community.

A CHAMPION IS DEFINED AS A PERSON WHO DEFENDS, FIGHTS FOR, or argues for a cause. Many people strenuously defend or argue for a cause, but we would hesitate to call them champions.

On this definition, Hitler would have to be characterised as a champion. To some people, no doubt, he is; but to the great majority of people in the world he most certainly is not. What is missing is a sense of morality and ethics; a lack of standards which others might seek to emulate.

The causes worth defending or fighting for, in the pursuit of which one might become a champion, are those which will benefit the greater good of the community. Once upon a time one might have said 'society', but that term has become so debased that nowadays it is used as a short-hand description of the prevailing ortho-doxies. In the Western world today, it would refer to those who subscribe to all aspects of economic rational-ism (which is truly economic determinism).

It's always possible to make things better. It takes a lot of effort, a lot of commitment, to stick to a vision that things can be better. It takes a lot of courage to stand up against sometimes entrenched attitudes and prejudices and biases.

Yet communities throughout the world suffer extreme levels of poverty and disempowerment in every way as a consequence of economic rationalism.

It's always possible to make things better. It takes a lot of effort, indeed a lot of commitment, to stick to a vision that things can be better. It takes a lot of courage to stand up against sometimes entrenched attitudes and prejudices and biases.

Of course, it is exhausting. But that's where one's life experience and strength gained from previous adversity come to the fore.

Perhaps there may be an obstacle in the way, but obstacles or problems are there to be solved. That's the challenge in life and I'm happy to be here facing that challenge. Of course, it is exhausting. But that's where one's life experience and strength gained from previous adversity come to the fore. If that's what championship is about then I guess we are all champions. Because I'm sure that we are all about making the world a better place than when we arrived.

In Australian society there's too much acceptance of the lowest common denominator, or mediocrity. We don't celebrate things like values and achievements. Neither do we promote them in our society. We occasionally make a token gesture towards them but not in terms of defining them and trying to promote them in the community. Are we able to nurture championship? I think this is a very necessary question for us to ask.

NELSON MANDELA

Icon of our times. No one alive commands greater respect. After 27 years in prison he emerged triumphantly to become President of a united South Africa. Nelson Mandela is the undisputed champion of the human spirit.

The self-belief of the champion must be tempered, he says, by respect for broader concerns.

THE 20TH CENTURY WAS IN HUMAN HISTORY THE ERA OF THE most outstanding and astounding achievements. Advances in science and technology outstripped the cumulative achievements of all previous centuries.

The limits of human possibility were radically re-defined as we made the far reaches of outer space accessible and penetrated the smallest units of matter. Communications and information technology shrunk the planet to a veritable village where the limitations of geographic separation became increasingly irrelevant for the exchange of knowledge and information.

In that situation of unprecedented progress and with the ability to transmit and share information across barriers and boundaries, one could reasonably have expected that human beings all over the world would have been living in conditions conducive to the fullest development of their potential. The contrary is, however, true; rather than humanity of the 20th century being a species of universal champions, the divide between those with privilege and those living in penury has increased.

The great arsenal of knowledge and capacity generated by the advances of the century was not effectively used to combat inequity.

We closed the century with an even more marked distinction between the powerful rich nations on the one hand and the poor and marginalised on the other. The majority of people on the planet continue to languish in poverty, subject to the social and physical degradation attendant upon poverty.

That the century closed in that manner is the more disappointing considering that it was also an era marked by the presence on the world stage of so many champions of freedom and equality.

The process of decolonisation, led by great fighters for freedom and dignity, was a major step towards global equality; the international community, once more under the leadership of some inspired statesmen, created bodies and agencies to guard over peace and freedom and protect the rights of all nations and people. As democracy spread to all parts of the world, the hope increased that the rule of the people would lead to greater prosperity and better living conditions for all.

How did we as a collective fail those champions of freedom, dignity and equality? Why did we fail to create the conditions for great achievement to be the domain of the many rather than a select few – the brave dream with which humanity entered the last century, one in which we all would have optimal opportunities to develop our potential to the fullest?

It is that relationship of the champion to the team, the leader to the collective, the achieving individual to the group and community that has occupied our attention throughout our life.

A recognition that no individual achieves and performs in isolation must stand at the heart of our reflections on what makes a champion. Those astounding achievements of the previous century we referred to are the products of the collective labours of human beings, at one particular point in time and as the cumulative effect of those of preceding generations.

I was singularly privileged by history and circumstance to have been in a position to make a particular contribution to what has been described as one of the great moral struggles of the last century.

A recognition that no individual achieves and performs in isolation must stand at the heart of our reflections on what makes a champion.

The fight to end apartheid and establish a non-racial democracy in South Africa captured the imagination and enjoyed the support of people from all walks of life in all parts of the world. That struggle on the part of the people of South Africa achieved championship status amongst the moral endeavours to make of the world a place of freedom, dignity and quality.

Those who were privileged to give leadership to that struggle and gain recognition in the wider world could only do so by the consent of the collective and through a respect for and acknowledgement of the collective efforts.

The necessary self-belief of the true leader or champion is tempered by respect for broader concerns.

No leader, no champion, who puts himself or herself above the people and above the team deserves that title or status.

This recognition of and respect for the collective inspires one to keep the common good constantly in mind. To achieve those goals to which one is committed and chooses to dedicate one's life, belief in yourself is essential. That self-belief becomes vain and egotistical, and ultimately self-defeating, if it does not derive from a dedication to and faith in the common goal. The necessary self-belief of the true leader or champion is tempered by respect for broader concerns.

We have learned through the experiences of our life that in all circumstances and in all communities there are to be found good men and women who are prepared to stand up for those common goals and to achieve for the common good. South Africa has provided an excellent example thereof.

When the rest of the world expected our country to go up in flames in the greatest racial conflagration ever, the presence of such men and women in all our communities contributed to a peaceful solution that is today described as a miracle.

In all circumstances and in all communities there are to be found good men and women who are prepared to stand up for common goals and to achieve for the common good.

The struggle to change South Africa was in the first place led by the liberation movement, but without the participation and cooperation of all the major political parties and the people of the country, such a peaceful negotiated political settlement would not have been possible. If our country achieved in the eyes of the world the status of a 'miracle nation', a champion nation of reconciliation, it was once more through the collective efforts of her people. Leaders and leadership were required to mobilise and direct those energies, but the energy came and derived from those good men and women to be found in all communities and groups.

Shall this century provide champions of human dignity and equality to match in their success that of the great innovators in the field of science and technology?

Twenty-first-century advances in learning and science will certainly be even more breathtaking in scope and impact on the human possibilities. Shall this century provide champions of human dignity and equality to match in their success that of the great innovators in the field of science and technology?

The commitment and dedication without which none can achieve and become a champion, need also in this century to be directed towards the betterment of the life of all people all over the world. While so many still labour under conditions where with the best will in the world greatness of achievement is out of their reach, those of us who do achieve find our rewards diminished.

It is fervently to be hoped that excellence of achievement and the dream of universal friendship will at last meet in this century. Let us be the champions of the ideal of making 21st-century humanity that species of champions: a brotherhood and sisterhood where all share in the fruits of our great advances and achievements.

GEORGE NEGUS

One of the most recognisable faces in Australia for his interviews with the world's greats – Margaret Thatcher, Bob Dylan and Steven Spielberg are all Negus interviewees.

Consistent with the style of his book *The World From Italy: Football, Food and Politics*, George's take on what makes a champion deliberately sets out to leave us with more questions than answers.

TO BE PERFECTLY HONEST, I HAVE CONSIDERABLE DIFFICULTY WITH the 'champion' concept. As a screaming egalitarian, it just doesn't rest easily. But having interviewed quite a number and a wide range of alleged, acclaimed, so-called or self-styled champions of one thing or another, the individual trait that stands out most – apart from the obvious areas of expertise, speciality and accomplishment – is their terrifying human ordinariness.

Ordinariness, an appealing first cousin to normality, and the second to humility, if they had it – was this characteristic. The so-called 'champions' in their fields who were also attractive individuals were almost without exception not exemplary but admirably ordinary. Celebrities who couldn't understand why they were; sportsmen and women who believed that their outstanding results came from hard work, not exceptional talent; academic innovators who recognised the essential worth of their assistants and colleagues; high-achieving business types who thought that providing jobs was at least as important as profit margins and shareholders; religious leaders who lived more in hope than in certainty; aid workers who did it because they realised somebody had to . . . I could go on, but a clear picture emerges to this old champion-watcher from way back of people who regard themselves as fortunate rather than special.

The individual trait that stands out most – apart from the obvious areas of accomplishment – is their terrifying human ordinariness.

I guess another way of expressing this scepticism is to say that I have always found the personae of so-called champions far more intriguing than anything that turned them into what society – Western society at least – has come to call a champion.

A few thoughts on this point. Ponder this list of people I have found myself chatting to over the years as a professional question-asker. Is Bob Dylan really a champion singer–songwriter or a champion protest stirrer? Is Margaret Thatcher a champion politician? Or more contentiously, is Margaret Thatcher a champion woman? Is John Elliott a champion businessman or a champion at getting into and out of trouble? Is Robert Redford a champion actor, a champion at looking like actors ought to look, or a champion environmental campaigner? Is Jim Wolfensohn a champion world banker or a champion, as Australians go, in international affairs? Is Martin Lee a champion Hong Kong Chinese freedom fighter or a champion human being? Is Eddie Murphy a champion funnyman or a champion African American? Is Romano Prodi a champion European or a champion Italian?

One man's champion could turn out to be another man's dead-shit.

What makes a champion? You tell me. You could argue that it depends on your working definition of the very word 'champion' itself. As depressing as it may sound, one man's champion could turn out to be another man's dead-shit. It is probably impossible to take ideological prejudices, behavioural psychology, private ethics and even personal partiality out of the 'champion' idea. 'He or she may be an exceptional whatever – indeed a champion whatever – but I can't stand his or her politics, let alone the way they wear their hair' is a tongue-in-cheek example of what a lot of champion ordinary people might say about a lot of champion extraordinary people.

I got the feeling that Nelson Mandela doesn't see himself as a champion – and that's what makes him one.

The 'what makes a champion' exercise that we were all involved in during Australia's Olympic year was lucky enough to have a champion by any standards or definition as its keynote speaker. It is international conventional wisdom not to say anything negative or nasty about Nelson Mandela. In fact it would take a champion nark to say anything that wasn't positive about this extraordinary man. But if I've got him right in his address, what he seemed to think made a champion was somebody who is intelligent and humble enough to use whatever they had that was exceptional to assist people who were not because of circumstances beyond their control. Unless you think this old hardhead is getting soft in the middle, that's a lot more profound than merely suggesting that we should take time to do things to help those less fortunate than ourselves.

I got the feeling that Nelson Mandela doesn't see himself as a champion – and that's what makes him one.

POPPY KING

Young Australian of the Year in 1995; a flamboyant symbol of youthful success who catapulted a cottage business into a world brand. She personifies commitment and staying power.

Ultimately, she argues, a champion is anyone who makes a difference.

A CHAMPION IS A COMPLEX AND UNIQUE MIX OF CIRCUMSTANCES and commitment.

Circumstances provide the element of chance that is present in all our lives. Often it is the desire to improve one's circumstances that motivates a champion. Sometimes it is the luck of circumstances that provides the platform from which to become a champion. Either way, the influence of our nature and the circumstances in which this finds itself is the fundamental starting point of a champion.

From there nurture takes over. A champion is someone who fosters their desire to achieve more than their fears. And that desire has to be fostered. It goes against human nature to face what is difficult. Our instinct is to protect ourselves from difficulties and it makes Darwinian sense to be so. However, a champion is someone who challenges this (for the people we consider champions are different from those we consider successful).

Successful is someone who has gone from strength to strength. But a champion is someone who has faced odds and beaten them. To do this takes extraordinary commitment to a level that is unusual.

In a group of people who set out to do a task, most will be eliminated at the first difficult post. A small group will keep going to the next post and so on and so on. It is the champion who will make it through to the end. That person does not give up, no matter how seductive and easy the idea to do so is. They have a different value system. They value achievement more than ease and have the commitment to see this through. Ironically, their ability to face difficulties becomes easier. But most of us never learn this because we give up too quickly.

Commitment is like a muscle; the more you use it the bigger it gets. Champions learn that the best way to make a fear go away is to confront it; it will never go away if you avoid it.

Our demons are often much smaller close-up than they are from far away and it is the people facing them that inspire us. These people are everywhere, not just in the boardroom, on the sporting field or in the media but in homes, schools and hospitals.

It is the people crazy enough to believe they can change the world who actually do.

You don't have to be on a world stage to be a champion; all you need do is make a difference. Progress relies on this and we rely on champions. For it is the people crazy enough to believe they can change the world who actually do.

SIR GUSTAV NOSSAL

Australian of the Year in 2000, he is a leading medical scientist and headed the prestigious Walter and Eliza Hall Institute for Medical Research from 1965 to 1996. Formerly Deputy Chair of the Council for Aboriginal Reconciliation, he is also Deputy Chair of the Strategic Advisory Council for the Bill and Melinda Gates Foundation Children's Vaccine Program.

Nossal's words provide penetrating insights into why he is a champion of science.

I WOULD LIKE TO BEGIN WITH SOME WORDS OF WISDOM FROM MY late 'boss', supreme Australian Science champion, Sir Macfarlane Burnet. When asked whether some important human trait was genetic or acquired, he would answer: 'Obviously it's 100% nature and 100% nurture!'

> *When asked whether some important human trait was genetic or acquired, he would answer: 'Obviously it's 100% nature and 100% nurture!'*

Innate ability alone is not enough. Obviously, the inherited endowment must be there. So, to a degree, I disagree with Allan Snyder. Gus Nossal tried for five years to learn the piano, but Gus Nossal could not have become Roger Woodward if he had practised for 50 years! The inherited endowment must be buttressed, augmented by a toughness of mind, a self-discipline, the will to be a champion, the strength to accept the burden of greatness. These traits of character will surely be shaped by life experience, by the environment if you will: family, social, cultural, educational.

Mentorship has been running right through our work like a golden thread – early mentors such as an inspiring teacher or an ambitious parent, formal mentors like a coach or a professor, informal mentors like a role model in one's chosen field whom one seeks to emulate. How important that we recognise, respect and reward the mentoring professions!

Yet good mentors alone are clearly not enough. Have we come any closer to defining or understanding that inner flame, the spark that marks a champion? We have talked about the commonalities: dedication, passion, commitment, discipline, persistence, sacrifice, Allan Snyder's champion mindset. But even more we have come to recognise the diversity of champions, a diversity so rich and varied that I fear the answer to Allan Snyder's question What Makes a Champion? will continue to elude us. Is that a worry? By no means, because we should glory in human diversity, the finest flowering of that bizarre but awe-inspiring phenomenon of biological evolution. What seems to me of supreme importance is not so much to codify the elements which make a champion, but to create a society where those with special abilities are recognised early, are encouraged, are given free rein to develop their talent and an opportunity to lead others along the same path.

Of supreme importance is to create a society where those with special abilities are recognised early, are encouraged, are given free rein to develop their talent.

In a country like Australia, with its engaging larrikin tradition and its rejection of class barriers, there is still a tendency to cut tall poppies down to size, with the notable exception of sport. Let me tell you about an interesting initiative of the Australian Institute of Political Science, known as the Tall Poppies Campaign. This is a program to popularise the work and the names and the lives of Australian science icons – the great traditional figures of history such as Florey, Burnet and Oliphant, but also more recent achievers. The idea is not to replace Don Bradman or Dawn Fraser in the pantheon but rather to allow the science heroes to stand beside them as a new group of icons with whom our young people should be more familiar. We recently announced the Cavalcade of Scientists – one from each decade of the 20th century – from Hargrave, the co-inventor of manned flight, and Mawson, the Antarctic explorer, to Graeme Clark, the inventor of the bionic ear, and Allan Snyder of optical fibre fame. We will shortly be launching the Cavalcade of Ideas to create a parallel set of icons from the humanities and the social sciences. We also have a Young Tall Poppies Campaign, which we hope eventually to run in each state. I might say that this initiative has been warmly embraced by both state and federal politicians, who realise the imperative need for Australia to continue to develop as the clever country, the knowledge nation. This celebration of Olympians of the mind can never be as popularly engaging as the Olympic

Games, but perhaps can develop in parallel as Allan has suggested.

We must also cherish the emerging champions among the first Australians – the Aboriginal and Torres Strait Islander peoples. We have already learned to honour the achievers in art, in music, in dance. We are learning to respect the traditional elders of communities who have the responsibility of maintaining the 50 000-year-old culture of their peoples. More difficult are our varied interactions with the newly confident and sometimes aggressively articulate political leaders of the Indigenous peoples who may threaten our comfortable self-image and even our vested interests. It is vital that the reconciliation debate so hopefully begun with these champions can be conducted with patience, compassion and mutual respect rather than being reduced to a media bun-fight of oft-repeated 15-second sound bites. There is also a great need to engage champion women in the fight against dysfunctionality in Aboriginal communities. Few things are more important as the still so very lucky country passes its Centenary.

Nelson Mandela defines the biggest barrier to world progress, namely poverty – the still struggling masses of people for whom human life is a struggle for survival. In this regard, out of our own self-interest and for the health of the planet, we must begin to behave like spaceship earth. My own expertise is in the health field, and I want to mention to you a hopeful public sector–private sector partnership between the major United Nations agencies (WHO, UNICEF and the World Bank) on the one hand, and a private sector foundation on the other.

I refer to the Bill and Melinda Gates Foundation, which has given over US$1 billion towards global immunisation, and in particular the purchasing of newer and more expensive vaccines for the 70 poorest countries in the world. I have the awesome responsibility of chairing the Strategic Advisory Group of the Bill and Melinda Gates Children's Vaccine Program.

Again inspired by Nelson Mandela, I will finish with a little story about what makes a champion nation. On 13 June 2000 in Oslo, the Prime Minister of Norway announced that his country was donating one billion Norwegian kroner to the Global Vaccination Program. Norway has only 4.3 million people, and this sum equals $200 million Australian. If we take it on a population basis, this is as if Australia had granted $800 million, or the United States had granted $12 billion.

These are sums to dream about for global public health – but really they are still basically affordable if Nelson Mandela's spirit ruled the world! Will you vote for Australia to be a champion nation in overseas development aid? This has been reducing on a proportion of GDP basis for at least the last 15 years, and is now at about a third of the level that the United Nations itself suggests is the appropriate sum.

We can all agree how enriching it is to hear some of the life experiences of champions in so many fields, how engaging it is that they can articulate their dreams and their fears so frankly, and how encouraging it is that so many of them want to help make Australia, and the world, a better place. For this we should all be truly grateful to Allan Snyder.

TAKING RISKS AND
BREAKING RULES

I confess to being a bit of a panic merchant ... I probably spend as much time worrying about things as I do actually getting the job done. The things I worry about usually turn out just fine. Does one really need the fear of failure at one's heels to succeed?

Bryan Gaensler

I was frequently afraid in moments of danger. If you're absolutely confident that you're going to overcome a problem, then why bother starting?

Sir Edmund Hillary

If you don't risk failure you will never succeed.

Anne Summers

That is basically the human tragedy: The comfort zone ... Don't let me think that I can do anything beyond what I'm qualified to do.

Bryce Courtenay

The true champions were the ones who had all of the other attributes but were also prepared, in the right circumstances, to break the rules!

Peter Ritchie

FIONA HALL

Singled out as Australia's pre-eminent contemporary visual artist, Fiona is the recipient of many prestigious awards, including the inaugural Contempora Prize. She is Artist in Residence at the Leunuganga Estate (Geoffrey Bawa's Sri Lankan estate). Her work crosses almost every medium imaginable and has been widely exhibited in London, Tokyo, New York and Berlin.

Fasten your seat-belts, she says.

THEY SAY THAT THE VISUAL SIDE OF THE BRAIN IS THE RIGHT HALF, but all of my ideas seem to come from 'left field'. Is this a perceptual collision course, or a state of perpetual malfunctioning?

The more careful – yet simultaneously more risk-taking – the better.

Being at cross-purposes or making some odd connections might have an important place in making a champion. The juggling act is between a logical mind and a reckless one. The more careful – yet simultaneously more risk-taking – the better.

But be prepared for some headaches.

SIR EDMUND HILLARY

The first person to set foot on the top of Mount Everest, enshrining him as one of the 20th century's great achievers. His feat, like Roger Bannister's historic four-minute mile, broke a mindset that said the great mountain could never be conquered.

Hillary's philosophy? If you know you can do it, why bother?

I'VE NEVER REGARDED MYSELF AS MUCH OF A CHAMPION IN the full sense of the term, be it in sports, the academic life or the business world. I've rarely competed with other people – my challenges have mostly been with the problems of nature that somehow I have to find the strength to overcome and where sheer survival is all-important.

Of course, I've watched many of the champions in action and greatly admired their skills. It is clear that the great athletes have sharper abilities and quicker reactions than the ordinary person plus a tremendous desire to win. They frequently have greater natural ability too than most of us will ever be able to emulate. I can only speak from my own experience.

But when you get down to it most of us are like me – you have to learn how to succeed. At high school I was tall and thin and reasonably strong but with little athletic interest, and every day I walked miles and miles just dreaming about adventure and the exciting things I'd love to do – but not actually doing anything at all.

> *I've rarely competed with other people – my challenges have mostly been with the problems of nature.*

When I was 16 years old I went with a school party to the mountains and for ten days I skied and clambered around in the snow and ice. It was the most exciting thing that had ever happened to me and it introduced me to a new way of life. Every spare moment for the next ten years or more I spent in the hills, and my skill and technique improved substantially. I revelled in new challenges – making first ascents of peaks and ridges (as was still possible in those early days). But I didn't regard myself as a champion – there were many other climbers of similar standard to myself.

I was frequently afraid in moments of danger, but I learned that fear could be a stimulating factor – it spurred me on to extend my abilities beyond what even I thought was possible. I learned much, too, from more experienced climbers and could swing my ice axe with the smooth skill of the expert.

> *I was frequently afraid in moments of danger, but I learned that fear could be a stimulating factor – it spurred me on to extend my abilities beyond what even I thought was possible.*

In 1951 four of us, all New Zealanders, organised an expedition to the Himalayas. Our skill with snow and ice proved invaluable and we made the first ascent of six summits over 7000 metres in height. Then two of us were invited to join the British Everest Reconnaissance expedition to the south side of Everest led by the famous British climber Eric Shipton. I proved to be the fittest member of the party and Eric took me under his wing. Together we climbed high on Mt Pumori to obtain the first ever view into the Western Cwm [cirque] and realised there was a potential route to the summit of Everest from this side. We made the first ascent of the formidable and dangerous ice fall but were ill-equipped to go any further, so we turned back.

Nineteen fifty-three was a great year for us. We were back on Everest again with a strong and experienced team and slowly overcame the many technical problems on the mountain – problems involving crevasses, ice walls, avalanches and bad weather. But we never thought of giving up. We established camp after camp and stacked them with all necessary supplies. Then we were ready for the final assault. Decisions had to be made to choose team members for the many demanding tasks high on the mountain.

There was little doubt about the summit team – Sherpa Tenzing and I had proved to be the fittest couple. We were extremely well acclimatised, and were strongly motivated too. With the support of our redoubtable companions we thrust upwards. I hacked a line of steps along the narrow summit ridge at 29 000 feet and at 11.30 a.m. on 29 May 1953 Tenzing and I stood on top of the world.

In a sense climbing Everest was a beginning rather than an end. I can clearly remember standing on top of the mountain with a warm glow of satisfaction and then looking across the Barun valley to the great unclimbed summit of Mount Makalu. Even while on top of Everest I mentally picked out a possible route to the top of the formidable Makalu. I had no sense of Everest being the end of things – it was just a stage to be overcome and there was still plenty left to do. After Everest the media immediately made us into heroes but I never accepted this. I knew I was an enthusiastic climber with a considerable desire for achievement and I was prepared to take a few risks now and then too. But a hero? No! Fitness and motivation had got me through.

> *I had no sense of Everest being the end of things – it was just a stage to be overcome and there was still plenty left to do.*

Not every hero is a champion and, of course, not every champion is a hero. It is often a judgement made somewhat irrationally by members of the public or media who may well have their own prejudices about what constitutes a champion or hero. Many years ago I made one of my first visits to Melbourne to give a lecture about the climb of Mount Everest. In those days I was reasonably famous. Next morning they arranged a taxi to take me to the airport. The driver was a rather tough and grumpy character.

'Your name's Hillary, isn't it?' he said gruffly. I reluctantly agreed this was true. 'You climbed some sort of mountain, didn't you?' he asked. I bashfully conceded that this was also true.

'I suppose it must have been tough going,' he acknowledged, 'but have you ever watched Australian Rules football? That's a really tough game!'

'I haven't watched an Australian rules game yet,' I told him, 'but I did have lunch yesterday with Ron Barassi.' The driver slammed on the brakes and turned around. 'With the Ron Barassi?' he exclaimed in distinct awe. I confirmed it was true. He gulped and fumbled for his small pad. 'Can I have your autograph?' he said. 'Geez, lunch with Ron Barassi!'

I started to follow a regular routine – a mixture of adventurous activities and aid programs. I drove three farm tractors with a New Zealand team all the way from the ocean across the crevassed Polar Plateau to the South Pole; I led my 'Ocean to Sky' expedition – driving three jet boats for 1500 miles up the great Ganges River of India from the Bay of Bengal to its wild source in the Himalayas; I landed with ski-equipped Twin Otter aircraft at the North Pole with the famous astronaut Neil Armstrong. But perhaps most important was the four-and-a-half years I spent with my wife, June, as New Zealand High Commissioner to India. That was a remarkable experience. And nearly every year I was back in the Himalayas climbing and building schools.

I had turned into an expedition leader and I learned a great deal about how to handle people too. What do you do if several of your colleagues are brighter and more intelligent than you are? To overcome this problem, each night as I lay in bed I calmly ran through in my mind all the possibilities that might occur over the next few days and worked out how to deal with them. If they did occur I was ready with an immediate answer. When a bright expedition member put forward an excellent idea that I hadn't thought of before, I wouldn't knock it back. I'd say 'great' and absorb it into my own plans and before long it would become my idea. So I learned to handle a vigorous and inventive team. I don't suppose we could be called champions but we carried out some mighty good projects in often dangerous conditions without any loss of life.

As I got older I became more involved in the welfare of the Himalayan people. My wife and I travelled around the world raising funds for projects for these worthy mountain folk. We helped them establish 30 schools, two hospitals and a dozen medical clinics. We constructed several airfields and at the request of our local friends we rebuilt Buddhist monasteries and cultural centres. I've been a reasonably successful adventurer and I've never lost a life, which I suppose is some recommendation. I've worked hard for the Sherpa people of the Himalayas and I've probably built more mountain schools than most people. If that makes me a champion then I'm happy to be called one.

Perhaps that's what being a champion is all about – regularly achieving what you set out to do.

So over the years I've done lots of expeditions and projects in remote areas of the globe – some big ones and lots of small ones – and most of the time I've managed to be successful. Perhaps that's what being a champion is all about – regularly achieving what you set out to do. That's the way I've always looked at it anyway!

FATHER BIENVENIDO NEBRES

Jesuit priest and champion of democracy, he became a pivotal figure in the ascendancy of Corazon Aquino to the Presidency of the Philippines. Now President of the prestigious and highly influential university Ateneo de Manila, he brings a unique perspective to the question of championship.

Taking risks and risking failure is the only way to achieve one's dreams, he says.

THE ATENEO DE MANILA HAS HAD A LONG HISTORY OF CONtributing to the education of leaders for the Philippines, including the national hero, Jose Rizal. A question we often ask of ourselves, therefore, is what makes a leader? I would like to write this essay on what I think makes a champion in the context of our efforts and reflections on educating our students for leadership and championship.

One of the aspects we emphasise is the importance of great desires. My colleague Fr Carmelo Caluag, S.J., speaks of pursuing a dream greater than oneself. In the language of Jesuit educational and spiritual tradition, we speak of the pursuit of the more, in Latin the *magis*. A question thus for us is how to motivate our students to aspire to great things and great deeds. What makes individuals aspire to be the best they can be?

But great desires are not enough. Over the years I have seen young people who have great desires, but they are either unable or unwilling to pay the price to achieve those desires. If there was one virtue I would wish to impart in abundance to them, it would be courage. By courage I mean the ability to take risks, or better to risk failure, as that path is the only way towards the achievement of one's dreams and great desires. Courage also means the ability to pick oneself up after failure and try again. How can we as teachers and parents impart courage, be supportive of our young people as they risk failure and as they fail? How can we assure them that it is OK and they can pick themselves up and try again?

> *The ability to take risks or to risk failure is the only way towards the achievement of one's dreams and great desires.*

As I look at those who have achieved greatly, one thing I have also noticed is they have continued to grow and continued to learn. I have noticed that it is not exactly a matter of talent. There are some with great talents who stagnate and cease to grow. There are others with seemingly lesser gifts who continue to learn and to grow and who emerge as the actual champions. Learning here is both learning from books and teachers and learning from experience and life, and bringing the two sources of learning together.

> *There are some with great talents who stagnate and cease to grow. There are others with seemingly lesser gifts who continue to learn and to grow and who emerge as the actual champions.*

In my own personal experience and in the experience of several leaders I know there have also been decisive moments either of failure or of high risk coupled with anxiety and fear, and in those moments they experienced the need to turn to spiritual resources. Among the Christians I know, we are surprised to find that we found ourselves turning to a similar event, entering into the experience of Christ in the Agony in the Garden, and finding strength in the faith that Christ himself experienced such terrible moments and that death itself can be faced with faith and courage. With younger people going through their own trials, I have found that better than giving them a lot of advice is to share with them that one has gone through such trials too, sharing how one went through them, and assuring them that it is OK; if they have faith and trust, their faith and trust will see them through.

If I may summarise then the aspects of championship that I have found important and that we would be interested in collaborative research on, they would be:

- How to inspire young people to have great desires, great aspirations.
- How to lead them through experiences that will gift them with courage, with the ability to take risks and to risk failure.
- How to help them recover and try again after failure.
- How to continue to learn throughout life, both from books and teachers, and from experience and life.
- How to find a spiritual resource that can see them through those decisive moments when everything seems to fall apart.

I would like to add special reflections on the question posed by Allan Snyder of 'God, Coach, or Country: who's responsible for your success and for whom do you do it?' 'Country' has been the dominant motivation in my own efforts and aspirations, whether in promoting education or in helping in political change. But it is God and my own spiritual tradition that has sustained me, particularly in moments of high risk and fear. And I have had the privilege of mentors along the way. Since younger days I have found an eloquent expression of my own beliefs in the credo of Dag Hammarskjöld, quoted in W. H. Auden's introduction to Markings. There Hammarskjöld speaks of service to one's fellow men and women as the noblest of aspirations. He goes on to speak of his source of inner strength, as coming from faith and trust in God. I resonate with the way he says that this faith and trust taught him the meaning of a love that found 'natural expression in an unhesitant fulfilment of duty and an unreserved acceptance of life, whatever it brought . . . personally of toil, suffering – or happiness'. Mentors (coaches) have also come who have taught me along the way. Some are heroes from our past, such as our national hero, Dr Jose Rizal. Others are teachers and elders who have shown me what it means to sacrifice oneself for others and how to live in deep faith and trust. I think in particular of a nun in grade school who told us countless stories of saints and heroes and through these stories taught me that the one worthwhile life is a life given for others. Her own life was also a witness of love and self-giving.

YIANNIS KOUROS

Renowned as the world's greatest ultra-marathon runner, Kouros is a perfect example of how sheer willpower and a preparedness to live dangerously can make a champion.

But, he says, from the moment you start to improve yourself you already have what it takes to be a champion.

IT IS NOT A DUTY, NOR AN OBLIGATION, FOR SOMEONE TO BECOME a champion, but it is a duty for someone to improve. From the moment a person wishes to improve, they already have the elements of a champion and are potentially a champion.

To me, you are not a real champion simply because you are gifted by nature or are provided with the genes. And you certainly are not a champion if you use illegal means to achieve something, regardless of whether you feel guilty or not. What makes you a champion is your devotion to the sport or field of interest and your hard work. It's your mental decision and attitude that makes the difference.

A good example is Jesus: if we accept that He was 100% God, we couldn't praise Him and say bravo because He rejected the offer of love from a woman like Maria Magdalene. But if we accept that He was also human, had human emotions and felt the attraction, but finally denied her, then we have the real meaning of effort. That's why He can be considered as a hero; because of His effort.

You can't admire and say 'bravo' to someone who is first in the world by doing easy things or doing things for fun, or because of genes and nature. You have to try hard, both physically and mentally; and then, if you are successful, you deserve to fly high in fame, glory etc. Glory, like all goods, has no meaning if it is given; you have to achieve and obtain something in order to feel satisfaction and pride; to feel that you deserve it.

> *You can't admire and say 'bravo' to someone who is first in the world by doing easy things or doing things for fun, or because of genes and nature. You have to try hard.*

I believe that nature does not endow with perfect abilities the person who is going to become a champion. This is so that the candidate has to find the self-confidence, do the necessary work and trial-and-error in order to discover those abilities and to become a champion.

On top of that, the feeling of the particular potential has not only to persist, but be reinforced with new discoveries and inspirational means. Work alone is not enough, but combined with intelligent ideas and newly discovered methods – which have been proven to work – the results can be miracles. Some people can do the above only through a mentor, a good coach or a guru-like teacher, a motivator. And some others struggle for years and knock on many doors, trying with passion to find such a person, because they believe that without this kind of guidance they are unable to get to the top.

True champions continue to realise their vision even when there is low encouragement or no encouragement, because they know how to find will, strength and energy from within. Beyond that, they also know how to become immunised against pain and sorrow. Even the most tragic event cannot interfere with their vision and cannot let them down, disorientating them from their expectations. Deep in their conscience is the fact that their zeal and devotion should be unshakeable.

In every field of cultural, sporting, technical or scientific activity, there are pioneers, who experiment, take risks and open roads for their successors. Successful pioneers usually become champions. Many people wish for such an opportunity, not just for the sake of the glory that an inventor receives, but for the knowledge gained through the challenges they went through and for the feeling of self-satisfaction for offering the world something very useful.

The characteristics of a champion begin with determination and with a thirst, full of endeavours and ventures, to achieve a goal. But the real champion is the person who brings together all their intellectual power to become inspired, the courage to endure as well as the physical energy. By summoning up everything, they strive for higher aims.

I could say that a person who becomes a champion is the one who does the following: makes the impossible possible, writes golden pages in history, achieves a lot under difficult conditions and pressure, has already achieved many goals and believes that they are still at the start, that they are still a student, and always learns from new experiences. A champion is the person who has faith in their own goals, dreams and visions through their own power and method; who is active and productive in their own field and contributes to the main community, who inspires a lot of people with their achievements to do better in their area, who chooses the uphill, difficult path, the hard work and the challenges that seem impossible to common people.

A champion is the person who strives to improve his own physical abilities and helps others to improve themselves; who is interested in the human mystery and man's innate strength to overcome all obstacles in order to find the hidden potential.

A champion is the person who is the unique star that sends light to their environment and makes people feel enthusiastic for something, making them think differently in order to approach a hard task with a lot of energy; the person who follows the Olympic ideals without being antagonistic – not to race against others, but against distance, time or other dimensions. A champion is the person who strives to improve his own physical abilities and helps others to improve themselves; who is interested in the human mystery and man's innate strength to overcome all obstacles in order to find the hidden potential; who feels during a hard task that they want to quit, but persists.

PROFESSOR GAVIN BROWN

Visionary Vice-Chancellor of the University of Sydney, and Chair of the Group of Eight elite universities. He is a distinguished mathematician who has held professorships at the universities of Washington, Cambridge and Paris.

Brown speaks candidly about life at the top of his profession.

WE WOULD ALL LIKE TO IDENTIFY THE COMMON FACTOR IN HIGH achievement across all areas of human endeavour, bottle it and make it universally available. Do champions really share some fundamental characteristic that ensures success, or must we match potential with the specific field in which it can be developed?

When I consider my own work as a mathematics researcher or as a university leader, the first thing that strikes me is the profound differences. I am Jekyll and Hyde – or perhaps Hyde and Jekyll. Certainly there are two profoundly different personalities and the transition from one activity to the other is profoundly painful.

Do champions really share some fundamental characteristic that ensures success, or must we match potential with the specific field in which it can be developed?

The researcher is a fragile flower-child, open and sensitive. Although the final product must pass rigorous analytical scrutiny the process of creating and discovering new mathematical insights is intuitive, incoherent and inarticulate. It is also exhausting. One's entire being must focus like a laser beam on a few constructs, but, simultaneously, peripheral vision is what admits the possibility of success.

The pure mathematician can be envied by the laboratory scientist because the former barely needs even pencil and paper. Mathematicians can work as well (sometimes better) lying on a sunny beach. This contrast misses the point, however, because it takes time to work oneself into the receptive state in which visions occur. The sly reference to religious ecstasy is deliberate, and I know many mathematicians who employ external aids to induce some form of heightened consciousness.

Very few can work at this intensity for long periods and the return to normalcy is a passage through vulnerability and sadness. The activity is essentially selfish, in the sense of self-centred, and, although there are many examples of fruitful collaboration, I believe these arise from shared insights when all parties report on their experience having 'come down from the mountain'.

All of this bears no resemblance to the life of a vice-chancellor, especially in today's business-engaged university. To be sure, in this role there is a need for a further personality split. The matters of true importance – research, scholarship and teaching – must be nurtured from a position of institutional leadership at the same time as a big corporate enterprise (in my case 5500 staff and 40 000 students) must be run efficiently.

Far from stripping away layers of protection to expose the raw creative inner self, one grows a carapace and needs a good dose of worldly cynicism to survive and prosper. It is not the challenge of unlocking one's own half-formed intuitions that matters. Rather one has the task of providing the environment in which many others are freed to achieve more of their potential.

The addictive reward is not direct personal achievement but achievement at one remove through enablement.

The job of a university CEO is perhaps the ultimate challenge of management versatility – 'a man for all seasons' – and no single person can have all the desirable skills. The broader the range of attainments, the more effective one is likely to be, and judicious shallowness may even be the job description.

By contrast, as I have said, the research mathematician depends on judiciously blinkered depth. Taking up one of the themes of Amadeus, one might cast Mozart as the mathematician and (a rather sweeter) Salieri as the vice-chancellor.

> The common feature possessed by all those whom I admire is ... a willingness to be confident outside the tribe. For this to be translated into achievement a degree of sheer bloody-mindedness is essential.

All of this may miss the point. I have described modes of human activity rather than criteria for success. The common feature possessed by all those whom I admire is self-referencing – a willingness to be confident outside the tribe. For this to be translated into achievement a degree of sheer bloody-mindedness is essential. Champions have the capacity for critical vision but it is their thirst to be doers that sets them apart.

KEVAN GOSPER

Vice-President of the International Olympic Committee and a Director of Shell International, he is a Commonwealth gold and Olympic silver track medallist over 400 metres. Transferring his brilliance from athletics to business, he went on to become Chairman and CEO of Shell Australia.

Here Gosper tells us that the most important dialogue to have if we want to be champions is with ourselves.

WILLPOWER IS THE MAGIC INGREDIENT IN THE MAKING OF A champion.

I don't subscribe to the view that champions are born. I've observed any number of individuals within society who start with modest qualities but by strength of character, sense of purpose, readiness to make personal sacrifice, alertness to opportunities, and the capacity to withstand mental and physical pain longer than their opponent, turn out to be champions in life whatever their chosen field.

While most champions normally benefit from either a special talent or an urge to pursue an activity in which they hope to do well, it is ultimately personal willpower which enables them to defeat or surpass all rivals in competition.

The decision, either sudden or gradual, to aspire to

becoming a champion is extremely personal.

It is, in Olympian terms, still today a quest for honour and glory, and yet every aspiring champion knows or learns that the way up is uncertain, tough, emotional and characterised by extremes of agony and ecstasy.

It is willpower deep within the very being of the individual that drives one to achieve the status of champion.

Winning is easy, losing not so. There are many crossroads that offer the aspiring champion the excuse to exit. It is willpower deep within the very being of the individual that drives one to achieve the status of champion.

I've learned that true champions are remarkably in harmony with their environment. They also possess within themselves a sense of balance and rhythm that to the observer renders their performance all too easy.

Nothing is perfect; nothing stays the same. A champion must listen and take advice but still be responsible for his or her own decisions. A champion never makes excuses, even though along the way mistakes are inevitable. After any reversal for any reason the champion must 'get back as soon as they can'.

There is deep in the heart of the champion not only the urge to reveal to themselves what they can do, but also the desire to offer inspiration for those around them.

The marks of a true champion are modesty and compassion, a willingness to encourage others, a desire to see their successors reach even greater heights than themselves.

The fundamental dialogue in life is the private one with oneself. It is within the secrecy of our own mind that we decide to compete, pursue a goal or focus on achievement.

We should be ever grateful in life for true champions in whatever field of endeavour. Champions move the world forward. They never give up.

PETER RITCHIE

He made McDonald's Australia the most successful branch in the world. His dedication to his workforce at home has produced leaders for the corporation around the world.

But, Ritchie says, it's imperative to start with the basics.

AT MCDONALD'S AUSTRALIA WE EMPLOY MANY YOUNG PEOPLE (50 000 in 2001) who, at least up to their mid-teens, are not champions. They seem to me to be a very representative selection of Australian teenagers (except maybe in their preparedness to work hard!).

Those who choose a career with us in most cases are turned into self-confident, capable people managers, and in some exceptional cases into real champions.

I am often asked, 'What is the secret to McDonald's training?' Australians seem to recognise that our stores do function smoothly and that we are able to provide outstanding attention to our customers, unlike many other retail businesses in the marketplace. (Parents are always the first to recognise the impact of our training on their son or daughter.)

There is nothing magical about our approach to training — it begins with a dedication to offering personal growth to all of our employees and is backed up by a substantial 'investment in people' and plenty of hard work.

The training is very basic in the early stages but progresses to very sophisticated psychological techniques as our young executives gain experience. (We have 22-year-olds running $9 million businesses!)

I often describe our basic training as a 'by the numbers' approach, and our critics have accused us of 'creating robots'. To some extent that is true, at least in the beginning, but I have found that young people almost always appreciate the need to develop a system in this way and as they become more self-confident they are able to inject some of their own personality into the most structured and mundane tasks.

What this process does, of course, is sort out those young people who are prepared to work hard and, most importantly, who can take their part as a contributing member of a team. (It is fascinating to watch how teams 'self-select' to ensure that each member is capable and 'pulling their weight'.)

As they grow in depth of knowledge of the system, leaders emerge, and we foster this emergence by offering opportunities for leadership-type courses to those who show an interest.

Now young Australian executives are in demand all over the McDonald's world – one of the many positives from globalisation? Australia is recognised as the most fertile country for growing young executives – the company has a young Aussie in charge of the whole of Europe, three others as Managing Directors of other countries and many others in senior executive roles within the parent company.

What is it that makes an individual capable of moving on from within the safe cocoon of the system in which he/she has been trained?

My answer to that question is that all of those individuals who we have, so proudly, been able to send out to the world have first of all developed a deep understanding of, and commitment to, our system, but then – and this is the key – have shown an ability to also think for themselves, to be very independent when appropriate.

The true champions were the ones who had all of the other attributes but were also prepared, in the right circumstances, to break the rules!

From those exceptional people we have had even more exceptional champions emerge, and during the 'What makes a Champion?' conference I was asked if there was one identifying difference that distinguished the 'true champions'. I thought about the individuals concerned and responded, almost instinctively, at the time by saying that the true champions were the ones who had all of the other attributes but were also prepared, in the right circumstances, to break the rules!

Having now had time to reflect on that answer, I would not step back from it at all; I would simply add that in being prepared to break the rules the individual shows his/her utmost self-confidence, knowledge of the system, ability to innovate, and, to some extent, that they have grown beyond the ability of their coach to lead them.

CAN WE CRAFT
A CHAMPION?

Are champions inherently brilliant? Apparently not. Many of the great minds of this world were average students. Neither Einstein nor Darwin was considered a remarkable student, yet both shattered the perceived wisdom of their field.

A 1998 study reported in Britain's Independent *newspaper followed the progress of gifted primary school children. It found that 'by middle age, all had failed to reach the top of their chosen professions'.*

There is an opportunity to create an environment where almost anybody can develop a champion mindset.

Imelda Roche

If this commitment to excellence can be inculcated in all aspects of our national life why should we not be a champion nation? For me this is the ultimate lesson of championship.

Jim Ferguson

Everyone is a potential champion.

Allan Snyder

PROFESSOR ELKHONON GOLDBERG

World-renowned neuropsychologist, his book *The Executive Brain: Frontal Lobes and the Civilized Mind* illuminates the part of the brain responsible for championship. He is Director of the Institute of Neuropsychology and Cognitive Performance in New York City.

What, he asks, is the neurological explanation for championship?

No MATTER IN WHICH ARENA YOU COMPETE, WINNING AND LEADERSHIP are a frame of mind. It is in your head. This is why it is important to understand the brain processes which ensure in some people the ability to compete, lead and achieve, and which malfunction in other people, leading to failure and defeat. The human brain is the most complex of all known organisms. It is the product of evolution spanning millions of years.

Of all the mental attributes, one trait is particularly important for success. Just as we recognise musical talent, athletic talent or mechanical talent, so too we are learning how to recognise the talent for leadership and achievement. A champion, a winner, a leader is able to focus on a goal, no matter how distant it may be, and to dedicate all his or her resources to that goal without allowing these resources to be diluted on trivialities. Of all the living creatures, only humans can set long-term goals and strive toward them despite incidental distractions, temptations and hurdles. We have the capacity to focus all our resources to attain this vision of the future. I believe that the extent of this ability, the capacity to focus all one's resources on a long-term goal, is what distinguishes winners from losers.

Complex neural machinery has developed to enable us to set long-term goals, to plan and to stay on track. This machinery is found in the front of the brain, in the so-called frontal lobes, and is the most uniquely human biological attribute. The frontal lobes, of the brain are often called the executive lobes, because they are to the rest of the brain what the corporate CEO is to a large company, the conductor to an orchestra, the general to an army.

Just as we recognise musical talent, athletic talent or mechanical talent, so too we are learning how to recognise the talent for leadership and achievement.

Neuropsychologists study the frontal lobes with the most advanced methods of neuroscience, to understand what it takes to be an achiever, what the brain mechanisms of success are. This has been the focus of my own work for the last 20 years.

As we learn more about the brain, mind-boggling possibilities arise. Soon it may be possible to identify leadership and achievement traits in people and to enhance them through our knowledge of neuroscience and neuropsychology. We are developing programs to attain these goals at the Institute of Neuropsychology and Cognitive Performance in New York City. The programs are designed to assess cognitive abilities with the most sophisticated neurometric and neuropsychological tools; to assist with employee selection in the business world; and most importantly to help improve cognitive abilities and mental fitness through the lifespan: in children, in adults and in the ageing.

We are also beginning to implement these programs in Australia in close collaboration with our Australian colleagues at the University of Sydney, Westmead Hospital and other institutions. As a frequent visitor to Australia, I find Australian neuroscience highly advanced and the overall environment conducive to innovation. My scientific collaborations with Australian colleagues have been highly gratifying and I look forward to future joint projects. We are finally beginning to understand the most human of all the human traits and to use this knowledge for helping people in the real world.

Before every success, there is a dream, a goal, a vision of the future. This is what the frontal lobes are in charge of.

It is not by accident that this event has been convened by the Centre for the Mind. Among the traits distinguishing winners from losers, the frame of mind is of foremost importance. It is all in your head. This means it is all in your brain. State-of-the-art neuroscience is beginning to home in on the brain mechanisms of leadership and achievement. The key seems to be the functioning of the frontal lobes, the most uniquely human part of the brain, appearing very late in evolution. Before every success, there is a dream, a goal, a vision of the future. This is precisely what the frontal lobes are in charge of.

JIM FERGUSON

Executive Director of the Australian Sports Commission from 1990 through to 2000. He has served as Australia's representative to the United Nations General Assembly, and as Ambassador to Peru.

If we can craft champions at the Institute of Sport, we can craft them in any field of endeavour, Ferguson says.

WE ALL KNOW MANY OF THE INDIVIDUAL QUALITIES THAT MAKE A champion, in sport or in any other walk of life. Dedication, hard work, the ability to overcome adversity, determination, focus, the ability to absorb pain and keep going, optimism and self-confidence are qualities demonstrated by all champions. In addition, of course, talent in one's chosen field might perhaps be regarded as a prerequisite, while an element of luck can be important.

The extraordinary person will always emerge, but if we desire to live in a champion country, or operate a champion firm, the occasional genius will not get us very far.

What is often neglected in this discussion is the environment that allows a person the chance to excel. I certainly do not mean that all champions have been favoured by positive or supportive environments. Many clearly have not. Witness Nelson Mandela, for example; although even in his case, the later man was undoubtedly shaped by his earlier environment. What I mean is that in our society an appropriate environment will provide more and better opportunities for people to excel, for champions to emerge. If we wish to produce champion scientists or pianists, or even champion athletes, we must develop the environment and the climate which will allow them to flourish.

The extraordinary person will always emerge, but if we desire to live in a champion country, or operate a champion firm, the occasional genius will not get us very far.

While in no way denying the importance of the qualities outlined above, the climate from which our champions emerge must be fostered. Although we would perhaps like to think Australia's success at the 2000 Olympic Games was something inherent in the Australian character or the result of being brought up on sunshine and Vegemite, we must recognise that, in reality, it was because we had developed a system to nurture our champions and encourage them to flourish. Plenty of athletes around the world live in fine climates and have good food. Most have similar physical attributes, talent and big hearts. Does it sound boring, that this great success was all the result of a good system, effectively managed? To me it is immensely exciting, because it is evidence that we can control our environment to produce success.

And, as it is true in sport, it is equally true in other endeavours, in the arts, in science and in business. It all starts with a commitment to the concept of excellence.

As President Kennedy is supposed to have once said, if you aim for second best you will end up second best. Champions do not aim for second best. Near enough is not good enough. But the commitment to excellence can only be realised through planning, from broad strategic planning down to personal organisation to ensure that no detail, however small, is neglected. It does not matter how big a heart you have. If you do not turn up for the race on time and well prepared you will not win.

Does it sound boring, that this great success was all the result of a good system, effectively managed? To me it is immensely exciting, because it is evidence that we can control our environment to produce success.

In preparing for the Olympics the Australian Sports Commission developed an overall strategic plan. All sporting organisations were required to develop strategies for their own sport. Each of these contained detailed organisational plans; to bring together coaching and all the necessary support services to ensure success. Coaches had their individual plans; each athlete knew precisely how they fitted into their teams and what they had to do. And this whole enterprise was driven by the commitment to do everything perfectly.

There should be no difference in any other aspect of our national life. Champion businesses do exactly what champion teams do. They have goals and strategies, they select their players and make sure they are skilled and fit, each player knows their role and what they contribute to the team. If this commitment to excellence can be inculcated in all aspects of our national life why should we not be a champion nation? For me this is the ultimate lesson of championship.

PROFESSOR
IAN CHUBB

One of Australia's most influential academics, Chubb is Chair of the Australian Vice-Chancellors' Committee, Vice-Chancellor of the Australian National University, and has served on various Commonwealth Government peak advisory boards. His research is in the field of neuroscience.

Every step we take to understand championship is a step towards a better future, Chubb says.

WE ALL THINK WE CAN RECOGNISE A CHAMPION. FOLLOWING great contests such as the Olympics, the newspapers are full of them.

But just what they are and what makes them remains an enigma.

From the medieval concept of the champion as one who fights on behalf of another or for a cause, a modern sense has developed of the champion as one who defeats all others in a trial of strength or skill and is open to challenge from all comers.

With the emergence of great figures who we recognise as champions, such as Martin Luther King and Nelson Mandela, something of the medieval concept is retained in the fact that their contests have been in great causes and on behalf of others. In sport the code of good sportsmanship also retains the element of acting on behalf of others, in that the function of role model is important.

We know a champion when we see one. They have often overcome great odds, either in sport or in political or social life – or have persevered against the odds until their goal has been achieved, as in the case of many of our scientific champions.

There is some intangible quality we recognise as making a champion. Most people would have sunk under the odds facing Nelson Mandela, but he emerged as a champion in the truest sense. We can see in him the same element of the extraordinary that we see in the many Paralympic athletes who not only overcame their adversity but also turned it into a matter for celebration.

Somehow their natural ability is connected to some other enabling factor that liberates an inner resource that lifts them above the common and labels them as champions.

Their motivation is important. Without motivation – the will to win, the desire to triumph, whether it be in personal performance or for a cause – the other attributes that contribute to the making of a champion are unlikely to prevail.

Whether it be a cyclist who overcomes cancer and physical debilitation to reassert pre-eminence, a politician who overcomes years of persecution to lead her country to reconciliation, a swimmer who takes his natural attributes to the peak and beyond, or a footballer who combines physical prowess with intellectual strategic ability, a key factor that makes the difference between a good performer and a champion is motivation. The same is true of the scientist who pursues inquiry, sometimes for many years, without any certainty of the outcome.

The speculation that they are tapping into some inner resource in the human mind that we are as yet unable to define is what has drawn the Centre for the Mind to ask the question 'What makes a champion?'

Universities and our society at large need all the champions we can get. Every step on the way to understanding just what makes a champion is a step towards a better future.

The Australian National University has produced many champions.

The ingredients in each of the champions are different in the eyes of most observers. The challenge for the Centre for the Mind is to discover what, if any, are the common characteristics and to find an explanation as to why those people in particular became champions. They will then explore whether there are ways of ensuring that we are all able to tap those attributes and to develop the ingredients in each and every one of us.

Universities and our society at large need all the champions we can get. Every step on the way to understanding just what makes a champion is a step towards a better future.

BRIAN SCHWARTZ

CEO of Ernst & Young, he has been at the centre of the Australian corporate scene for more than twenty years. Schwartz has championed a 'people first' work environment that saw Ernst & Young named as one of Australia's top twenty-five employers.

He believes a 'people first' culture will bring out more champions.

THE QUESTION OF CHAMPIONSHIP IS AS RELEVANT TO THE BOARD-room table as it is to the sporting field or the science laboratory. But while we are accustomed to celebrating our sporting heroes and honouring our scientific gurus, we are somewhat less accomplished at recognising and encouraging those people among us who demonstrate championship behaviours in business. Even so, it is invariably those who display what we might call 'championship characteristics' who have the capacity to lead, inspire and provoke us to greatness, no matter what our field of endeavour.

So what makes a champion in a business sense? And how do we recognise and encourage such behaviours so that they spread like a virus to all elements of our organisations?

To me, championship behaviour in business must be evident not just at the leadership level – because there can be no question that that is critical – but at all levels throughout an organisation. Champions' behaviour challenges existing systems and structures; champions delight in finding new and better ways of doing things; they commit to innovation and ongoing change and they inject enthusiasm and excitement into the work environment. For business leaders, the challenge lies in creating a culture that supports such championship behaviour among individuals while at the same time nurturing other valued behaviours such as teamwork, efficiency and a commitment to quality.

> *Champions' behaviour challenges existing systems and structures ... they inject enthusiasm and excitement into the work environment.*

One of our chief goals at Ernst & Young is to create a 'people first' culture that recognises the value of all our individuals and seeks to empower them to reach their full potential within our firm. We see the two defining characteristics of a 'people first' organisation as the creation of a high-performance culture where individuals know they are paramount to our overall success, and the development of an environment where our key focus is to help our people build their skills, market value and relationships.

In my view, initiatives such as these are critical to recognising and encouraging championship behaviours at all levels in business, so that the individual desire to innovate, challenge and solve does indeed spread like a virus throughout an organisation, creating a championship culture for business.

GENNADI TOURETSKI

One of the world's great sporting coaches. His protégé swimmers Alex Popov and Michael Klim were ranked world numbers one and two for the decade of the 1990s. He is a driving force behind the success of the Australian Institute of Sport's swimming team.

While anybody can be a champion, he says, the process of crafting one is like cutting a diamond.

MANY THINGS ARE INVOLVED IN THE MAKING OF CHAMPIONS; many influences and forces. Twenty years ago, what made champions in Russia was politics as dictated by the Department of Propaganda of the Central Communist Party.

During the Cold War, competitions aimed to reflect the power of various countries. Was it good for sport in the USSR? Very good. Was it good for sport in the world? I think so. Sport became a message of peace and friendship. But in my early days, sport was a patriot game.

Society and geopolitics are, however, changing rapidly. Now it is the worldwide media, rather than politics, that seeks out and promotes champions. Whether this is good or bad, we must accept that it is so. For an athlete, however, the most significant motivational factor remains the honour of representing their country.

I believe the process of crafting a champion is very similar to that of producing diamonds. You can find a precious stone, but you must cut it for it to have value.

While I was a successful swimmer, I never thought I'd be a coach. As a schoolboy I wanted to be a molecular biologist; as a university student, an expert in hydrodynamics and bionics. The important thing I got from university was that I met people there who taught me to learn from them and helped me to open my creativity. My father, a military scientist, said, 'I understand what you are doing at the university, but if you want a career in science, be sure to be a military man. You need to have access to secrets. If you do not, you can be smart, but . . .' He was right. Finally he said, 'You are a celebrity in sport − you should take to this area.'

When you train elite athletes you should not dominate. You must give them the freedom to be themselves, to explore their own potential.

When I started, I was coaching kids who were seven to nine years old. My question to myself was whether I could give my heart to them. Or would they irritate me? Am I a giver or a taker?

It took me a week to work it out: my heart belonged to them.

When they're kids, you must be ahead of them. You have to tell them what to do. When you train elite athletes you should not dominate. You must give them the freedom to be themselves, to explore their own potential.

For example, one of the swimmers who came to me didn't have the psychological characteristics of a champion. He was good, but his coaching regime had not allowed him to develop anything but an inferiority complex. I said to him, 'You can do it this way or that. But what do you want? What is your goal?'

At first he attempted to talk a lot to me. But I had more experience. I knew that the more you talked the less success you had – the steam goes to the whistle. Eventually we established a level of communication where we understood each other with no words. We concentrated on developing unbeatable fitness and technique, and international success came soon.

But I think championship is in the mind, rather than the body. I divide body types three ways: poles, triangles and cubes or squats. Alex Popov is a pole, slim and tall. Michael Klim is cube-like and Matthew Dunn is triangular. These three world-record-holders have absolutely different personalities and different physical types. But they are all great champions.

I believe it is possible for us to produce in every child of every person a celebrity in some field or another.

The thing they have in common is that they have strong motivation, which allows them to do a lot of work. However, they are sensitive to different types of instruction. What is good for Alex is not good for Michael, and what is good for Michael is not good for Matthew. A coach must understand this and adjust training programs to different people.

In spite of all the perfecting and analysis of technique,

I still think the psychology of a champion is the most important thing. The ability of a competitor to focus on the goal and remain free from distractions is a major characteristic in a champion's personality.

Forbes Carlisle said many years ago that we must develop environments that can produce champions. As head coach of the swimming program at the AIS I set out in 1992 to create a team of champions in order to create super champions.

I believe it is possible for us to produce in every child of every person a celebrity in some field or another, using a sporting or educational environment based on understanding that everyone can be a champion.

Most people are born with talent. The mission and the challenge of a coach and educator is to recognise this talent.

DAVID MOORE

One of the great post-war photographic artists. His photographs have been published in *Life*, *Time*, and *Fortune* magazines, and are among the collections of the Bibliothèque Nationale, the Museum of Modern Art, and the National Gallery of Australia.

Belief in a beckoning future, he says, is the springboard for excellence.

IN ANSWER TO THIS INTRIGUING QUESTION I WOULD NOMINATE THREE essential ingredients: talent, creativity and perseverance.

Talent – the raw quality that is intrinsic or inherited, producing a degree of superior performance.

Creativity – an ability to see outside the box of accepted achievement and standards.

Perseverance – a commitment to making the apparently impossible possible.

If talent is not part of the make-up of an individual their chances of supreme achievement are lessened. When creativity exists questions can be asked about the extent of the possible. Perseverance is the engine of achievement which can overcome obstacles.

The mind that can seize on an opportunity is one step closer to a goal. Also, those who turn adversity to advantage see positives where others see negatives.

For the gifted, dedicated achiever, barriers are often transparent walls capable of being shattered.

Perhaps most importantly the potential champion needs to possess the seemingly contradictory characteristics of humility and ego.

Entrenched conservative society erects barriers. The status quo is a powerful restraint to visionary concepts. Yet for the gifted, dedicated achiever, barriers are often transparent walls capable of being shattered. A belief in a beckoning future is the springboard for excellence.

ROD MACQUEEN

The envy of every Rugby Union nation in the world, he assembled and coached an Australian rugby team described as the best ever. How do you coach a good team to become undisputed world champions?

It begins, he says, with standards.

SUCCESSFUL TEAMS ARE ALL ABOUT STANDARDS. EVERYONE HAS GOT standards. It just depends how high they are.

The art of management is to bring a group of people together and unite them in a common cause. There is no doubt that there is a very similar analogy between sporting teams and business. We're bringing people with different skills and attributes and attitudes together and channelling them to a common cause and a common goal; uniting behind a set of standards.

When you unite behind a set of standards or common cause, there is a sacrifice to be made. You must sacrifice individuality to achieve the team ethos. If you think of yourself, you only worry about yourself and the team will never come first. The team must always come first. Sometimes it's easy to achieve the team ethos, but even for the best of team players sometimes it needs to be manufactured, and this is something a good coach is always on the lookout for.

Any great endeavour will involve good times and bad times. When things are tough, all that means is that there's a gap in standards that has to be filled – a period of time until you're going to be the team that can be the best. How long it will take to achieve that standard is the question.

The worst thing a coach can do is to make excuses for losses. It's better to assume that you lost because the other team was better and you did something wrong, even though luck may have taken a part in it. If you don't allocate responsibility to luck, then you don't allow luck to take a part in losses. But good luck may be cultivated – and cultivated through correct preparation.

Provided you are refining your technique and leaving no stone unturned in your preparation, you are on the right track. With enough determination and preparation, teams and individuals reach a state of 'flow'.

There is a big difference between practice and correct preparation. You can practise many, many times but you could be practising the wrong things. Striving for perfection is what championship is all about. For example, a boat crew may spend hours every day on the water practising, but not improving their technique. That crew is bound to be reasonably successful because, even though they are doing the wrong things, they are doing them together. However, that crew will never be as good as the crew that puts the same amount of time into refining their technique. Provided you are refining your technique and leaving no stone unturned in your preparation, you are on the right track. With enough determination and preparation, from time to time teams and individuals reach a state of 'flow'.

Many people are interested in the concept of 'flow' or 'the zone' in sports – that time when a team or a player operates with seamless precision, without thinking. I see that there's no mystery to it. Sportspeople and teams are constantly seeking perfection. Flow has got to happen eventually because if you strive for the very highest standard you possibly can all the time, if you're never content with not having those higher standards, eventually those standards come together – the iron filings line up and a state of flow is achieved.

So what makes a champion? A mindset that says there is always a way and that never accepts otherwise. If your opponent is clearly better and clearly beats you because they are better, you know that tactically you might be all right but you've got a lot of improvements to make and that's going to take time. If you accept and identify that, you'll still end up winning. If we are striving all the time, even if we don't become champions, we'll never be average.

PAUL BATCHELOR

As CEO of the AMP group of companies, he plays an industry leadership role as a member of the Business Council of Australia and the Treasurer's Financial Sector Advisory Council.

His secret? Helping people succeed.

BEING A CHAMPION SEEMS TO COME EASILY TO SOME PEOPLE. THEY are the individuals who are born with the innate will, talent and drive to succeed.

The bigger issue for societies and organisations is understanding how we can enable otherwise 'ordinary' people to achieve extraordinary things.

> *You could argue it is even more important, from an economic standpoint, to build champion businesses rather than champion sports teams.*

We can do it. The desire to excel resides in all of us. In that sense, everyone has the potential to be a champion. The challenge lies in realising that potential and learning how to succeed.

Understanding the factors that nurture and amplify great achievements is as valuable for business as it is for sporting teams, artists, scientists and adventurers. You could argue that it is even more important, from an economic standpoint, to build champion businesses rather than champion sports teams.

Helping people succeed is fundamental to the success of any organisation. That means creating the right environment to enable talent to flourish, innovation to prosper and our people and the business to grow together.

This is the essential element in creating truly 'champion' Australian organisations.

MARK BAGSHAW

Paralysed at age 16, he must be the most senior Australian corporate executive with a severe disability. Bagshaw is the International Marketing Manager for IBM Australasia, Chair of the Australian National Training Authority's Disability Forum and co-founder and Chair of the Ability Australia Foundation.

Along with personal drive, societal influences will craft a champion, he says.

I'M A RARITY IN OUR COMMUNITY. IT WOULD APPEAR THAT I'M one of the few people, if not the only person, in a senior executive position in Australian business with a severe disability. That makes me unique but it doesn't make me more special than anybody else.

In fact I think there are four elements that make a champion. I've always been a person with drive and I used that drive in my early days. I had my accident when I was 16 years old; I dived into shallow water and broke my neck. Up till that point my mother would describe me as a difficult child. I was a handful. I was always trying to push the limits on things and there was every chance that I would have used that drive to go off on the wrong path. I was coming close to doing that at 16 years of age. I was close to being expelled from school, and those sorts of things. I wasn't the worst in the world but

I was certainly pushing the limits. At 16 I was presented with the challenge of dealing with a disability and I think I used that drive to overcome, at least initially, some of the effects of that disability.

Family support, I've always felt, was an essential part of this so-called championship that I experienced.

Apart from personal drive, I think there are three other elements in making a champion.

The second element is the right family environment. My family demonstrated something to me that I don't see in most families and communities. A message: 'Mark, we're here to support you,' and secondly, 'We expect you to put some effort in to make this happen.' And I wonder, when I look at championship, if I might be in this sense the embodiment of that particular championship that's helped me personally get to where I am. The people around me, particularly my sister, are at least as much champions as I am. But they will never be recognised. So that family support, I've always felt, was an essential part of this so-called championship that I experienced.

The third factor is the support that I got from the community. I got the right support at the right time from the community to get me to Sydney Uni. The Commonwealth Rehabilitation Service was the embodiment of the community support for me to help me overcome those infrastructure obstacles. I think it was all of those things combined that have helped me overcome the adversities of a disability.

I was lucky to be in the right place at the right time. It might sound odd to say that, and certainly I wasn't in the right place at the right time the day I dived into the water, but I have subsequently been very, very lucky.

And the fourth element – and it is absolutely crucial – was just that I was lucky to be in the right place at the right time. It might sound odd to say that, and certainly I wasn't in the right place at the right time the day I dived into the water, but I have subsequently been very, very lucky. For example, coming to IBM, a company I didn't even know, just before I'd finished university to apply for a job. The only reason I applied for the job with IBM was that they'd given me a typewriter two years earlier and it had an IBM logo and I thought if they gave me a typewriter they might give me a job. That was good luck. And subsequent to that I have been, several times, in the right place at the right time.

IS THERE A CHAMPION
MINDSET?

Roger Bannister broke the elusive four-minute-mile barrier, thought by many at the time to be a physiological impossibility. He then went on to a distinguished career as a neurologist, becoming Professor of Medicine at Oxford. Is a champion mindset transferable?

No matter in which arena you compete, winning and leadership is a frame of mind. It is in your head.

Elkhonon Goldberg

What makes a champion is a champion mindset. The champion mindset is the transferable commodity, not the skill itself. If you have done something great in one field, you are far more likely to do it in another.

Allan Snyder

It is a mindset that says there is always a way and that never accepts otherwise.

Rod Macqueen

The greatest thing that is achieved by the Olympics is its enduring capacity to turn on the light in the brain of a young child anywhere in the world — tens of millions of them. The young child who resolves to become a swimming champion and ends up being a great film director.

Peter Montgomery

HERB ELLIOTT

Arguably Australia's finest athlete, his brilliance continued in the corporate sector. He became a household name in 1960 when he won the 1500 metres Olympic gold medal by a record margin of 20 metres. He went on to be Chief Executive of Puma in the United States and Director of Athlete and Corporate Relations with the Australian Olympic Committee.

He suggests that the journey to championship may only produce humility.

THE INGREDIENT I DON'T UNDERSTAND IS THE INGREDIENT OF desire. Desire that is so strong that it will not allow compromise and entices or drives the champion remorselessly and inevitably to championship. It has to be available in sufficient measure to take a person through boring daily routines, doubt and distraction. Why do some have it but most don't?

Resisting the small insidious compromise is the maker of champions, and giving in is the destroyer of those that might have been.

The champion understands that small compromises, so small that they are evident only to them, are not small compromises at all: they are a decision to concede on championship and slip back to the rest of the field.

Resisting the small insidious compromise is the maker of champions, and giving in is the destroyer of those that might have been.

The path to follow is well trodden and well understood by all.

- Have a powerful desire to get closer to perfection.
- Have enough intelligence to select (maybe with some help from a mentor) the process that is going to take us closer to perfection. This process or route has to be in tune with what we are physically, mentally and spiritually, or our efforts will wane.
- Recognise that many people get this far but can't hack the boredom of sticking to it in every action every day, so it's not going to be easy. Trying to get closer to perfection every day is exciting and boring at the same time.
- Revel in doing it because it is tough. Don't look for the easy way.
- When you can't go any further is when you have the opportunity to break new ground and move into the championship zone. Champions are never incubated in a comfort zone.

If we want to be the best then we have to be the best at each of the component parts. Identify the component parts and deal with them one at a time until no-one is better than you in that component. And then move on to the next.

All this is known. The journey makes us more aware of our weaknesses than of our strengths, so it is a journey that if properly travelled should breed a humble champion.

YVONNE KENNY

One of the most accomplished sopranos of her generation, she made her operatic debut in London and has performed as a soloist in the world's most prestigious opera houses.

Here she discusses commitment, dedication, purpose and generosity of spirit.

WHAT MAKES A CHAMPION? WHAT'S THE DIFFERENCE BETWEEN a high achiever and a champion? I've been thinking about this because I for one certainly don't feel like a champion as I'm still totally immersed in the process of learning my craft, improving and refining my technique and trying to realise my potential. Every time I go on stage I think to myself, 'OK, this time I'll get it right. Maybe this'll be the one.' This focused desire for that unobtainable perfection keeps driving me forward with total determination to the next goal and the next goal and I guess I'm never satisfied. That's what the journey feels like from the inside. It doesn't feel like championship at all. It feels like a constant striving to improve – to go one better than the last performance.

I think the irony is it's other people who observe these journeys we are making and determine who are the champions. The quality of championship is observed and bestowed by others from outside the actual process.

> *To have the courage to honestly explore and understand yourself, to face your own demons that are always lurking in the back of the mind and waiting to pounce at a vulnerable moment. This understanding of self is vital to self-confidence.*

There are so many elements for us to consider which are part of the journey. There's the obvious basis of a natural or exceptional talent but it must be backed up by an ability to optimise the talent through hard work and training. A single-mindedness to the exclusion of nearly all else in your life. A determination to keep going when it's not working so well – to bounce back from the knocks; to turn problems into advantages. I think most importantly, the process of self-examination. Nelson Mandela touched my heart when he mentioned that 'it's easy to change your community but the hardest thing is to change yourself' – to have the courage to honestly explore and understand yourself, to face your own demons that are always lurking in the back of the mind and waiting to pounce at a vulnerable moment. This understanding of self is vital to self-confidence and self-belief. But it's also about dreams. It's about having the courage to follow that dream at all costs. It's totally compelling; there's no choice. Perhaps following the dream in the imagination is really creative visualisation.

The power of the mind over the function and biochemistry of the body is extraordinary. There are amazing discoveries being made in the area of mind–body medicine. Is it the power of thought that gives the body the competitive edge? Or is it inspiration from a spiritual force: a god; a faith?

True champions are the few who have the ability to excel at the moment of the most extreme pressure ... true champions are those who display humanity and humility and a generosity of spirit.

We join together to explore all these ingredients which contribute to achievement of excellence. There are the obvious visible rewards for championship in our society. The Nobel Prize, Wimbledon, the Booker Prize, the World Cup, the US Open, the Bledesloe Cup, an Olympic gold medal. True champions are the few who have the ability to excel at the moment of the most extreme pressure. Inevitably, there is always an element of celebrity attached. Yet true champions are those who display humanity and humility and a generosity of spirit in helping those following in their footsteps.

However, to me, true championship extends far beyond that. It means being a compassionate human being. It means those who selflessly and anonymously give their time and their energy to helping others who are less privileged. It means those who dedicate their lives to selfless service of their fellow human beings, to fighting oppression, to sacrificing their own wellbeing for an ideal or for the common good. It means those who fight to maintain and preserve our natural world environment in the face of the ravages of modern life.

What makes a champion? It's difficult to qualify and quantify because it all comes back to the indefinable quality of the human spirit which rises up at the moment of challenge or adversity and propels our great champions, in all areas of human endeavour, to feats of great courage.

BRYCE COURTENAY

World-famous for his international best-seller *The Power of One* (adapted for the screen in 1992), he is Australia's best-selling author. His other titles include *The Potato Factory, Smoky Joe's Cafe* and *The Family Frying Pan*.

This former advertising executive says that the journey rather than the trophy is what's important.

BEING A CHAMPION TO ME HAS NOTHING TO DO WITH HOLDING a trophy above your head. It has everything to do with getting involved and persisting, often hanging on for dear life.

> *To use your imagination, to dream what might be and then to power the dream with persistence; that's what makes a champion.*

We have been given the gift of language, and with the gift of language comes the gift of imagination. What we can imagine, we have the power to achieve. Most people use this very power to imagine the consequences of what might happen if they tried to do something unusual. Rather than visualise a successful outcome, they fall short before they even start. That is basically the human tragedy: the comfort zone, don't move me beyond it, don't let me think that I can do anything beyond what I've been qualified to do.

Champions are always prepared to do the hard yards, to live the lonely hours, to take the flak, and most of all to break the rules.

To use your imagination, to dream what might be and then to power the dream with persistence; that's what makes a champion. The trophy is the destination, it's not the journey. The dream is the journey. Dare your genius to take that journey. Champions are always prepared to do the hard yards, to live the lonely hours, to take the flak, and most of all to break the rules.

DR IAN GAWLER

One of Australia's best-known long-term cancer survivors, he lost a leg to bone cancer in 1975. A recurrence of the condition led to his ground-breaking development of mind–body techniques in a Western medical environment. As the author of four best-sellers, his work has expanded to focus on broader issues of health and wellbeing.

Champions, says Gawler, are remembered not for the records they break but for the values they embody.

CHAMPIONS HAVE THE ABILITY TO BLEND THE POSSIBLE WITH THE impossible. In doing so they achieve extraordinary results.

True champions rise above their achievements and make their mark on history by displaying exemplary human values. Champions embody the qualities of hope, love, faith, wisdom and compassion.

Champions retain an exquisite capacity to be able to act appropriately in the moment. This often leads to behaviours that could well be described as paradoxical. Single-minded persistence one moment, letting things go the next. This is the quality of discrimination, the capacity to know what works best in a given circumstance and the flexibility to act accordingly.

How do we recognise a champion?

Presence: You feel a champion's presence often before you see or hear or touch them. They exude a quality that is at once reassuring, reaffirming, comforting, securing. It is a good feeling that needs no other explanation.

Communication: A true champion communicates directly – either by word or deed. There is something obvious they communicate that speaks clearly and directly to us about the best of human values. They leave us feeling as if we have gained something – learned something, clarified something. We are left with a clear knowledge that this something is of great value.

Position: A champion has a clear opinion and is forthright in expressing it. This opinion is likely to be blessed by wisdom and compassion and be readily accessible. Again, it will be meaningful.

Champions are held in high regard because they offer hope, inspiration and instruction. Their achievements and qualities inspire us with what we may be.

When we go beyond the literal performance of a champion what is really on offer is a model for how to be, rather than how to do. When we aspire to be our personal best, it helps us to overcome those tendencies of laziness, hopelessness, pessimism. If our lives are touched by a champion, the power of the mentor may work its magic and help us to embrace our full potential.

> *When we go beyond the literal performance of a champion what is really on offer is a model for how to be, rather than how to do.*

In Herman Hesse's book *Siddhartha*, the hero, an aspiring holy man, clarifies what he has learned through many years of ascetic studies and practices. He describes what it takes to achieve remarkable results:

'It is what fools call magic and what they think is caused by demons. Nothing is caused by demons; there are no demons. Everyone can perform magic, everyone can reach his goal, if he can think, wait and fast.'

I believe within these three words – think, wait and fast – lie the keys to the champion's performance. What then is their full meaning and how can we develop them?

To my own understanding, thinking in this sense requires that we recognise three principles of positive thinking:

1. *Developing a clear goal*

Mental clarity is a major requirement for peak per-formance. This can be learned through mind training and meditation. Mind training in logic and deductive thinking harnesses the capacities of our formidable intellects. Meditation frees us from limited perspectives bound in the past and the future, frees us to soar in the creativity and immediacy of this very moment.

In utilising mind training, decision-making based upon the efforts of the intellect offers one level of con-fidence. Intuition adds the power of inner conviction. The two together provide the clarity that gives unshake-able confidence to goal setting.

Inner conviction combined with sound reason trans-forms belief into faith. Belief is a deductive process. Based upon the probabilities and possibilities, we believe something to be possible. We can have a weak belief with strong doubts, or a strong belief with few reservations.

With belief, however, there are always doubts and with them comes a fear of failure and a need to protect ourselves against those doubts. Faith knows no doubt. Faith is certain.

Interestingly, with this commitment to the goal comes a flexibility with the means. Champions have the capacity to hold to a long-term goal in a way that is uncompromising, yet they experiment with, reassess and modify the means by which they achieve that goal.

There is a final question about the source of clarity and commitment so highly valued in positive thinking. Where does it really come from? Is all this the manifestation of an obsession and so to be regarded as some sort of pathology? Or is it something more powerful? Perhaps a delight in talent and human performance is a healthy manifestation of an uncomplicated human being?

It could be either and most likely is a mixture. In youth, high achievement often rides upon the aspirations of parental projections, the need for external approval, the hope of filling an inner void. People who really succeed in life may well have had a mixed motivation to begin with but through their experiences learn transcending values and so find a sustaining inner peace.

2. Doing whatever it takes

Total commitment, perseverance, and personal control. It is easy to identify the qualities of those who get things done. They all add up simply to doing whatever it takes.

To develop these qualities, as Hesse identified, the capacity to wait and the capacity to fast are keys.

To wait means to be patient; to persist with humour and a good heart.

To fast means to go without. Literal fasting (i.e. going without food) has been a constant recommendation in all spiritual traditions and is highly relevant in any contemporary life. Champions may well need to go without a variety of other things to reach their specific goals.

3. Choose to enjoy doing it

Recognising what choices they do have is a hallmark of champions. They know that they cannot always choose what they are required to do. Sometimes events and circumstances conspire in a way that apparently offers little choice. It is as if life itself required that certain demands be met.

Champions recognise that they have one inalienable right – the right of deciding how they choose to respond to that demand.

Sometimes champions can be observed laughing at the demands placed upon them. Sometimes they are awed, even really scared. Often they are delighted to be in such a position. Whatever the response, the champion knows that they have the freedom to choose their response – and that they are capable of following through with that choice.

> *What will matter in 500 years' time is how we lived. What values we aspired to, how we expressed those values and what legacy we passed on for future generations.*

Remember, it does not matter anyway. In 50 years' time, the athletic records of today will be a matter for old memories; in 50 years' time, current business performances will be of little consequence. In 500 years' time, all this will be confined to dusty records, most likely of scant interest to anyone.

What will matter in 500 years' time is how we lived. What values we aspired to, how we expressed those values and what legacy we passed on for future generations.

True champions will be memorable, will be worth remembering, because of the values they embodied. These great souls are the ones who hold the virtues of hope, faith and love alive today – and offer this gift to the future.

IMELDA ROCHE

Bill and Imelda Roche established Nutrimetics (Australia) in 1968. By the early 1970s the Roches had expanded the business into Asia and the Pacific. In 1991 they shattered a national mindset when the Australian 'branch office' bought out the US-based parent company. Roche has served as an Australian representative to the Business Advisory Council to APEC and is the Chancellor of Bond University.

Just one of her messages: if it is to be, then it is up to me.

THE QUESTION WHAT MAKES A CHAMPION? IS FASCINATING to explore. Is it the pursuit of an ideal, a vision, a dream to the exclusion of all distractions, the ability to overcome, to endure, to sacrifice, to stay focused? Is mental stamina as crucial as or more crucial than natural attributes and physical ability, and do champions emerge in fields of endeavour other than sport – such as architecture, science, literature, business, agriculture, academia, music and the arts? Must champions be winners, set records that others must measure themselves by, or is it enough to be considered a champion – to be outstanding in any chosen field of endeavour?

There is no doubt in my mind that not everyone can be a champion in the universally accepted sense of the word. Our society tends to confine the accolade of champion to only the most distinguished sports achievers, giving minimal acknowledgement to the broader scope of championship. It is easy to recognise physical achievement – championship of the mind is far more elusive.

It takes a confluence of elements (I will comment on these a little further on) to achieve championship status in any field of endeavour. Even with the presence of all the necessary elements, would a champion basketballer become a champion cricketer or would a champion golfer become a champion tennis player? Although all of these sports demand well-developed ball skills, they are not easily interchangeable at championship level because they require such specific and focused development. This can also be true of intellectual championship.

I believe that the human brain is hard wired from birth to accommodate human frailty as well as strength and our inherited gene profile creates individual potential. However, what happens from birth to maturity to enable that potential to develop to its optimum is greatly influenced by environment and nurture.

A champion acknowledges and accepts that 'if it is to be, then it is up to me'.

Whilst engaged in the What Makes a Champion? event, the following themes were, in my view, continuously reinforced.

- The essence of championship is having the determination to be the best we can possibly be – this takes commitment, effort, sacrifice and single-mindedness.

- A champion mindset is one that embraces a 'can do' attitude even when tackling the unknown or the previously unachievable.
- A champion acknowledges and accepts that 'if it is to be, then it is up to me'.

For Australia to develop a championship culture in its broader sense requires of us to provide opportunity, and appropriate education and training, in an encouraging environment together with a healthy dose of nurture to enable our young to develop the confidence and self-esteem necessary for a champion mindset – or to become a 'champion'.

Few individuals achieve championship status without a support network of committed people.

In an ideal world Australia would be among the global leaders in embracing a national goal to ensure that these elements should not be beyond the realm of possibility for the majority of our children to tap into. Both physical and intellectual championship require nurture and discipline, commitment, dedication and expert coaching. Few individuals achieve championship status without a support network of committed people.

Australians are both obsessed with and entertained by a huge variety of sports and have a well-developed culture of recognition, hero worship and support for our sporting champions (and our entertainers), but not for our academic, scientific and business champions. I believe our nation could do with some attitudinal rewiring.

It would serve us well as a nation if we were to lose

some of our entrenched 'tall poppy' negativity and our willingness to dismiss or ridicule the vision and aspirations of others while offering no better thoughts, actions or solutions – and our attachment to the belief that much virtue lies in being an ordinary Australian. What could possibly make being ordinary attractive?

Is it the handy comfort zone we hide in and use as a shield, when we are not prepared to be challenged or to challenge ourselves? Is it a product of laziness or lack of self-esteem? Is it the fear of not being accepted by others – the fear of risking failure or ridicule? Fear can be a more powerful motivator than recognition. At the same time we should also recognise that it is human to seek and enjoy recognition. Recognition is a powerful incentive and motivator, even for champions – perhaps especially for champions.

> It would serve us well as a nation if we were to lose some of our entrenched 'tall poppy' negativity and our willingness to dismiss or ridicule the vision and aspirations of others ... and our attachment to the belief that much virtue lies in being an ordinary Australian.

Australia needs to mature its attitude towards championship and excellence in the broader sense, beyond sport, and recognise that high achievers, whatever their calling, expand the playing field and create opportunities for others. Wanting to build platforms for success is a very desirable mindset as even the smallest achievement can constitute the first platform.

Life could ideally be likened to a golf game, where we constantly play against our own handicap in a companionable social environment, versus say the comparative solitude of distance swimming or marathon running. Golf stands above the rest because it provides frequent sociable pauses after each shot (read effort/achievement) and though we most often play in pairs or fours, we compete as individuals playing against our own handicap.

My invitation to participate in What Makes a Champion? would not have been extended if the Centre for the Mind was not focusing on the broader definition of champion, and its linkages. Which brings me to the question, Is leadership a form of championship? Does effective leadership require a champion mindset? This is a subject in itself which I will not attempt to explore here, except to say that preparation for sporting champions usually begins early in life as soon as natural abilities are recognised, whereas leaders often emerge later in life, drawing their strength, vision and motivation from experience, circumstance and events.

While there are skills and attributes leaders and champions often share, the primary focus of championship versus leadership is different. Champions must focus on achieving their personal best to the exclusion of others whereas leaders must embody values that can be shared by others. Leaders must be capable of thinking collectively while acting individually and in the interests of the group. Leaders are recognised for their personal qualities and their ability to influence the performance of others. The goal of leadership is to bring out the best in others.

Both 'champions' and 'leaders' are achievers. Both are inspirational – capable of inspiring others to greatness.

RALPH DOUBELL

Gold medallist at the 1968 Olympic Games whose winning run set an Australian record (which still stands), an Olympic record and an equal world record. He then went on to Harvard Business School and has been a leader in the Australian business community ever since.

Doubell's description of his gold medal win at the Rome Olympics shows the adversities that can strike even at the threshold of triumph.

WHEN I WAS ON THE BLOCKS FOR THE START OF THE 800 METRES Olympic final on 15 October 1968, the runner next to me broke.

As we lined up for the restart, the judge pointed to me and warned in a very clear voice that if I broke again, I would be disqualified.

My immediate challenge was to stay calm and remain focused on my race plan and its outcome. To be distracted by an official's mistake was a threat.

At that moment, the outcome of the Olympic final hinged on my mental toughness, not on my physical ability.

I had trained to be as strong and as fast and as fit as I could be. But outstanding physical fitness, speed and ability are common features of all Olympic finalists.

*At that moment, the outcome of the Olympic final hinged
on my mental toughness, not on my physical ability.*

My strategy was simple – start slowly, stay out of
trouble throughout the race, maintain contact with
Kiprigut (the favourite, and in my mind my main competitor), and then kick on the final bend. The start,
therefore, was not critical. I knew my start was not going
to determine the outcome of the race.

I was able to ignore the official's error. I had a vision
and a hunger to win. I had also executed my race strategy perfectly in the heat and semi-final on the two
previous days. I knew I could do it again. I had come
there to win.

For over five years I had developed, with my coach, the
vision of winning. We shared that vision. On 15 October,
the day of the final, we could clearly see that the Olympic
final was going to be a two-man race. I had beaten
Kiprigut, both physically and mentally, the day before in
the semi-final. I knew I could do it again – with the same
strategy. But execution of the tactics required real mental
toughness. The key difference between champions and
competitors, at this elite level of performance, is mental
toughness.

I think champions develop a vision of winning and
the mental toughness to be totally focused on their vision.
Champions have a hunger – be it economic, or for status
or a need to be the best, or whatever else – to win. Champions have the ability to maintain focus and withstand the
mental pressure of competition.

JOHN EALES

Considered the greatest rugby union player ever, his magnificence on the field was matched by his leadership of Australia's most successful rugby side.

How can this giant of an aggressive contact sport also be famous for being such a nice guy? Perhaps it's the very thing that enables him to be a champion.

I'VE ALWAYS CONSIDERED MYSELF TO BE VERY FORTUNATE. THE biggest fortune that I've had is the upbringing or the environment that I was brought up in.

I was one of six kids. My parents showed their support for us, whatever we did. It was unconditional. They may not have agreed with what we did at different times, but as long as we weren't going to harm ourselves, they'd let us make our own mistakes.

My parents encouraged us in our endeavours whether they be academic or sporting. They created an environment in which we weren't afraid. It didn't matter to them if we made mistakes, they'd still love us at the end of the day.

When I was at university, I had no idea what I wanted to do. I got reasonable marks, but didn't dedicate myself that much to my studies. I was enrolled in a psychology degree and also did human movement studies.

After a year, I still didn't know what I wanted to do. So I made a decision to do only that which interested me and changed to an arts degree. Of course, I was always keen on sports, and rugby was one thing that interested me at that time, but I didn't dream I'd be able to go as far as I have.

What motivates me is to be as good as I can be. In terms of rugby, I want to have left my mark as someone who was able to add something else to the sphere that I was in. But rugby has a time limit on it. It's finite.

Being part of such a winning team in rugby, however, has given me the experience of success.

I'm sure there is a champion mindset. I can perhaps describe it as a mindset that blots out all else apart from the goal or task at hand. A person who has a champion mindset believes they can achieve against everyone else's expectations. I think the champion mindset is developed, rather than an inherent characteristic in a person.

You don't want to be really successful at something and then never be really successful at anything in your life again. The beauty about life is there are a thousand challenges out there. We've just got to pick one challenge at a time and work on it.

> *I'm sure there is a champion mindset. I can perhaps describe it as a mindset that blots out all else apart from the goal or task at hand.*

The model that my parents have shown me – let your kids make their own mistakes; give them encouragement; let them know you love them regardless; and also try to show them success as well – I believe is a big contribution to nurturing a champion mindset.

> *Let your kids make their own mistakes; give them encouragement; let them know you love them regardless; and also try to show them success as well.*

TRIUMPHING OVER
ADVERSITY

Winston Churchill had bouts of severe depression throughout his life, which he called 'my black dog depression'. Yet he rallied a nation to triumph over the extreme adversities of war.

Lance Armstrong is a triple Tour de France champion. Before his 1999 victory in the most gruelling of cycling events Armstrong had overcome testicular cancer, which had spread to his abdomen and brain in late 1996.

Recovering from failure is a most important quality.

Kevan Gosper

That's the mark of success — to make it look easy when it's actually unbelievably difficult.

Bryan Gaensler

CORAZON AQUINO

Former President of the Philippines. The assassination of her husband propelled this senator's wife to world prominence. Not defeated by his death, she rallied the nation to end the 20-year dictatorship of Ferdinand Marcos, becoming a symbol of hope for the people of the Philippines and for men and women around the world.

She says it was simply a sense of duty to a cause that compelled her to act as she did.

WHEN I MET PRESIDENT MANDELA HE HELD NO TRACE OF bitterness at all. He exuded peace. He is a man who, in spite of all his suffering, maybe because of his suffering, has arrived at the stage of peace, and who could inspire others to work for the peace which has eluded so many of the peoples of the world. My husband and I always believed that his imprisoned years were the greatest learning experience of our lives. And without that experience I don't think, speaking for myself, I would have been able to accept losing my husband under such treachery and also having the guts to challenge a dictator.

Prior to my husband's imprisonment, he was sought after by many people. When he was a Senator of the Republic, many people thought that he would become President. Afterwards you suddenly realise that you have very few friends or you have very few real friends. And then things that mattered before do not seem as important. You go from being the wife of a Senator who is highly respected and who comes with many friends, and then suddenly people are just avoiding you. It seems as if nobody wants to see you, or everybody is afraid to even be seen with you. So I didn't think highly of our compatriots.

But if my husband had not been in prison I would not have discovered my hidden strengths; they would have forever been hidden.

Very few people knew me when I was Aquino's wife. Suddenly the whole world got to know me when I became his widow. I returned to the Philippines from Boston three days after his assassination and the following day we accompanied my husband's coffin to the church. The day after that I thought I'd go early to church so I could at least look at his body again. When I arrived there were just such long lines and I was worried as I was by myself. I said, 'Excuse me, I am Corazon Aquino, I am his wife.' And the people there said, 'Oh, she's Aquino's wife, let her through.'

> *If my husband had not been in prison I would not have discovered my hidden strengths; they would have forever been hidden.*

It felt great that people who had never met my husband were taking the time, maybe risking the ire of the dictator (Marcos), by standing in line and just wanting to have a glimpse of him. You could say that that was one of my great moments: the sudden realisation that 'my husband was right, these people are worth dying for'.

I realised Filipinos appreciated my husband's sacrifice after all, even if they had kept quiet for all those years.

I think the one quality, the one trait that I would look for in a champion would be selflessness. And it does not matter from what culture you are. I mean you think of Martin Luther King, Nelson Mandela, I think of my husband, there is one quality they all possess in common which is the forgetting about self, just thinking of others.

I look to Jesus Christ as my model. And definitely he cared not for himself but for the people. And so to be a champion, for me, is to think of the good of others, and not just of oneself. So that would be my definition of a champion: one who is willing to risk anything and everything for the cause.

Whenever I'm asked, 'Why did you do that?' I say: 'I believed that it was the right thing to do regardless of the consequences.' When challenging the dictator no-one assured me: 'Cori, all you have to do is challenge him and we'll be there with you.' I just believed that I could make a difference. And that I would perhaps have felt guilty about not doing it at the time.

I had never had any ambition to become President. But it was my duty. My husband and I were committed to the cause of democracy. My husband had died, and it was impressed upon me by many of the Opposition leaders that I could unite the Opposition.

I was thinking, 'Haven't my husband and I done enough?' In fact, my oldest daughter asked: 'Mom, haven't we suffered enough?' And so I said: 'Well, I used to think that each of us has a quota for suffering, at least I wanted to think that. But apparently things are not like that in this world.'

My definition of a champion: one who is willing to risk anything and everything for the cause.

When I returned to the Philippines and came face to face with my husband's lifeless body, I promised him I would continue in the struggle to restore democracy. At that time I did not know what that would entail. After my husband's funeral, the demonstrations and the protest marches began. I was leading the women most of the time. But beyond that I was not thinking of myself as being a politician.

Ultimately, I went into the battle. I knew I had a chance but that the chance was minimal. But I had to try, because I would never be able to face myself or free myself of guilt if I had not even tried to make a difference. I have a favourite quote: 'I am only one, but still I am one. I cannot do everything, but still I can do something. And so I must not refuse to do the something that I can do.' Maybe this is what I was thinking about when I challenged the dictator.

In fact when I'm before a group of women I say: 'If you want a formula to becoming President, I'm afraid I don't have that because an assassinated husband would have to be part of the formula.'

I think, all over the world, women have not been given the opportunity. It has been a given that men perform better, although I don't know who gave that idea. We women have still had to prove ourselves. And it is only now, at last, that women have been acknowledged as being as capable as the men are. But even when I was studying in the United States, I guess the men always had a decided advantage over the women, and to this day

America has not produced a woman President, so at least we beat them to that.

Because of all the crises during my husband's imprisonment, during his 40-day hunger strike, during the time that he was brought to another military camp, I was made to believe that he had already died. And then came the realisation that you can't really count on too many people.

Of course, I had a high every time thousands of people would be shouting out my name. I would admit to really having highs. People would tell me they derived strength from me but I felt I was the one deriving strength from them, especially during my husband's funeral. If all the two million that they estimated to be there had not gone there, I wonder if I would have been as courageous as I was.

If I were to meet a great champion I would ask them: 'What do you think you can do to produce more and even greater champions? Can this be taught or is it really a matter of having role models as the greatest teachers?'

Is there something that we can teach or does it need to be experienced, and not just learned from books? It is in adversity. Sometimes you have someone who you think of as a hero, but when a crisis comes you think, oh he wasn't a hero after all, or he wasn't as great as I thought he was. So I think the ultimate test would be how a person ranks in times of suffering, in times of great trial. Forgive my immodesty, but I think I passed some of those trials.

> *Is there something that we can teach or does it need to be experienced, and not just learned from books? It is in adversity.*

I came face to face with Nelson Mandela, who had spent years in imprisonment, as had my husband. If you have endured all this suffering you emerge a greater person than you were before. If you did not believe in an Almighty, if you did not believe that there is life after this, that there is justice – somewhere, maybe not in this world but definitely in the next – you could not survive.

PROFESSOR PETER DOHERTY

Nobel Prize laureate in the field of medical research, he is Chair of the Department of Immunology at St Jude's Research Hospital, Memphis. Professor Doherty is strongly motivated by the belief that controlling diseases like AIDS and malaria will contribute enormously to sustainable development throughout the world.

Quitters never win, Doherty tells us.

THE PHILOSOPHER LUDWIG WITTGENSTEIN TAUGHT US THAT LANguage defines perception. Language is built from words, so we had better know what the words mean. Webster's dictionary gives three definitions for 'champion':

1. The holder of first place or the winner of first prize in a contest, especially in sports.
2. A defender, advocate or supporter of a cause or another person.
3. One who fights.

I expect that there are elements of all these in a champion (the winner, the advocate of the defenceless and the general good, and the warrior). Many of our sporting heroes are contemporary warriors.

Words are built from letters. Scientists like me are game-players. Here is one version of a letter game for 'champion'.

C   is for courage. It takes guts to focus on the tough and difficult. If everyone can do it, there can be no champion. The idea of a 'champion toothbrush user' is absurd to anyone but an advertising executive.

H   is for hutzpah. A variant of the Yiddish 'chutzpah', meaning brazenness, or pushiness in the Australian vernacular. The shrinking violet may be beautiful, but the flamboyant rose is arguably the champion of all flowers.

A   is for application. Anything that is worth doing demands concentration and diligence. Here we may distinguish the 'winner' from the 'champion'. The most indolent of us can win the lottery but would only achieve champion status if, for example, the wealth is used for some general good.

M   is for madness. More than a little insanity is required to spend five hours a day in training, or 16 hours in the laboratory. We could call this the Van Gogh effect. Some of the most inspired people I know survive on the edge of dysfunction and breakdown. The truly sane are content, live less intense lives and spend more time at the beach. Triathlon athletes also spend time at the beach, but they must be at least a little crazy.

P   is for persistence. Quitters never win. The dilettante who hops from issue to issue can be an interesting companion, but will never be a champion.

I   is for integrity. The champion who cheats, and is

found out, is soon destroyed. Even genuine heroes have to be very careful, especially in Australia, where the 'tall poppy' is always at risk of being lopped or flattened. We are not unique in this: Abe Lincoln, Martin Luther King and John F. Kennedy were all shot.

O is for originality. Champions in the arts and sciences are celebrated for presenting something that is genuinely novel, or for illuminating the familiar in a way that is different and intriguing. The originality of the athlete may be in some physical achievement that looks so extraordinary that none would have thought it possible.

N is for nobility. Being a winner is great, but it takes generosity of spirit to be a true champion.

Who has shown greater nobility than Nelson Mandela?

We could play the same game again with: creativity, humanity, altruism, magnificence, passion, insight, optimism and nonpareil. Nonpareil? For those who are not familiar with the word, alternative Webster definitions are 'without equal' and 'a small flat chocolate drop covered with butter'. It seems to me that many of our champions are like that: extraordinary in one dimension but low-key, familiar and even trivial in others. In short, real heroes are flawed and human. Could a being who is so superior that nothing seems to require pain or effort appeal to us as a champion? The champion has suffered, endured and overcome.

> *It seems to me that many of our champions are like that; extraordinary in one dimension but low-key, familiar and even trivial in others. In short, real heroes are flawed and human.*

All of us can be champions within our own heads, which may be a good thing for our psychological well-being. However, it is doing, not thinking or talking passionately with friends, that makes a champion. The champion has to be 'out there' and visible. The term 'compassionate conservative', to borrow from election rhetoric in the USA, is just a cynical sham if the true meaning is 'I feel and understand your pain, but it's your problem.' Empathising with the plight of the poor and the suffering is fine, but hollow in the absence of action.

> *It is doing, not thinking or talking passionately with friends, that makes a champion. The champion has to be 'out there' and visible.*

We must collectively face the fact that at least 800 million people do not get enough to eat each day. The plant breeder Norman Borlaug won the 1970 Nobel Peace Prize for triggering the green revolution. He is now 86, still works at the Institute in Mexico where he did his pioneering studies, and spends much of his time trying to convey the message that the application of conventional plant-breeding techniques alone cannot possibly satisfy future global food requirements. Borlaug's active research career was funded by the Consultative Group for International Agriculture Research (CGIAR), an organisation that was put together by an Australian champion, Sir John Crawford.

The International Rice Research Institute of the CGIAR achieved a major increase in rice production in India by distributing an improved, conventionally bred variety. Do we, however, want to slow future progress by limiting access to the newer and more powerful technologies? Saffron rice has been engineered by a Swiss group to prevent vitamin A and iron deficiency, prominent causes of blindness (in children), anaemia (in women) and death in countries that rely on rice as a major staple. What if we can modify bananas to deliver an AIDS vaccine, or even an AIDS drug, to help combat the current catastrophe in Africa? The potential for human good is enormous, though the application of genetic modification technology must be carefully monitored for both human and environmental safety. We need champions in the media who will continue to promote rational debate in this complex area. It is essential those in government keep the international aid dollars flowing for GM research by not-for-profit organisations like the CGIAR. The potential benefits must be freely available to all.

The recent peacekeeping initiative in East Timor showed that this country has the compassion and the maturity to champion the cause of the oppressed. We saw champions from all nations emerge, and be celebrated, in the Olympic Games. This is a good time and place to focus on what it takes, in the broadest sense, to promote a culture of heroism and extraordinary achievement.

DR ANNE SUMMERS

Journalist, editor, author and social commentator who is most widely known for her best-seller *Damned Whores and God's Police*. Summers was editor of Fairfax's *Good Weekend* magazine, and of *Ms* magazine in New York. She is a Walkley Award winner for journalism, served as head of the Office for the Status of Women, and was an adviser to Prime Minister Paul Keating.

Here she examines the unique preoccupation Australians have with success – and then failure.

A CHAMPION IS SOMEONE WHO IS WILLING TO STAND APART FROM the crowd in order to achieve his or her chosen goal. This can often mean isolation and loneliness, feelings that may even be exacerbated when the goal is reached and the champion is even further removed from the lives of everyday people. In Australia, we are suspicious of champions unless they are excelling in sport – and even then we only like them while they are on top.

Australians tend to undervalue achievement. Although we adore our sporting heroes, we're terribly mean to heroes in other areas. So the whole question about where championship, where excellence or accomplishment comes from is a difficult debate to have in this country. We think our sporting heroes were born with it because it seems so easy when they win. Everybody else has to go overseas to make a mark, and if you come back we hate you; if you stay over there we like you as long as you don't criticise us.

To have failed at a business or to be sacked from a job or to have had a marriage fail makes you deal with an issue that there's no preparation for. No-one ever teaches you how to fail. I'm not sure that we're taught how to succeed either but there are plenty more models around for success than there are for failure. We are pretty tough on people who we judge to have failed, and I think that is something we need to address. We need to say that people can come back, people can reinvent themselves.

> *We are pretty tough on people who we judge to have failed, and I think that is something we need to address. We need to say that people can come back, people can reinvent themselves.*

I was in business in New York for a while and that business failed. I came back to Australia and I was interviewed live on ABC radio. The interviewer asked: 'What does it feel like to be a failure, Anne?' And I said, 'Well, I don't feel like a failure. I feel like I've had an extraordinary adventure, and, OK, it didn't work out but I feel that I learned a lot from it.' And this person said, 'Well, you would say that, wouldn't you?' Australians adore failure in certain fields – for example, military – but we don't like it in other fields, and it's a kind of a national ambiguity I guess about how we deal with success or failure.

I also think we need to encourage people to succeed in lots of different areas. Just because you're good at one thing it doesn't mean you can't transfer that skill to another area. But what worries me still about the sporting mould is that it's so easy to measure success because there's somebody who wins, or you beat your personal best; whereas in other fields it's sometimes very hard to measure success.

Achieving the goal is almost secondary to the mental and physical discipline and strength required to make the decision to go for that goal.

JEFF HEATH

He has triumphed over physical disability and societal attitudes. When many wheelchair users were living in institutionalised environments, Heath attended university and hitchhiked around New Zealand for fun. He represented Australia at the 1976 paralympics, and is an activist and the editor of *Link* magazine.

Enthusiasm and opportunism, he says, are key ingredients of championship.

IN MY LIFE I'VE DONE WHAT OTHERS HAVE SAID WAS, IF NOT impossible, then highly unusual. In the 1970s I attended my local high school, represented Australia at the Canadian Paralympics, went to university and hitchhiked around New Zealand. All while using a wheelchair. The following decade I travelled extensively, driving a motor home across the USA, researching a book in the Pacific Islands and teaching English in Japan. My biggest professional challenge has been a two-decade involvement in the Link disability magazine.

In the modern world our first thoughts of a 'champion' tend to be of those with exceptional skill who have succeeded in their chosen field – usually on the sports field. But historically a champion is also a person who fights, or argues for a cause or on behalf of another; a person who battles for another's rights or honour. In both cases, a champion is someone who will achieve what others said was impossible. Defining what a champion does is relatively easy. Understanding a champion's motivation is not as easy.

It has been said that I fit both definitions of a champion – one who is successful in my chosen field and a strong advocate for all those with a disability. If I am really typical of a champion then I think a recent incident may shed some light on the motivation of a champion.

To celebrate the 20th anniversary of Link I sought an interview with the Prime Minister. Knowing he would be in Adelaide in mid-August, I suggested that date – without success.

On the proposed interview date, in Adelaide I passed a man standing on the road while coming down a side street. He was well-built, wearing a suit, and he was waiting for something to happen, rather than waiting to cross the road. I almost missed the coil of wire coming from his left ear and disappearing inside his coat collar. 'Perhaps he is a bodyguard,' I thought – not a common sight in Adelaide. I further surveyed and saw another 'spook' and two well-dressed women whose stance and clothing said 'ministerial minders'.

I concluded that the Prime Minister must be coming to this very side street imminently. Within five minutes the PM drove up.

I made eye contact, smiled and gave a nod of recognition. Twenty seconds later he agreed to an interview when we were both in Sydney – he to open What Makes a Champion?, me to participate.

Champions respond to stimuluses by creating an excited explosion of neurons that produces links and pathways that are hard to keep up with. A champion may start at point A but they rarely go to point B. Instead they head off to wormhole # and on to parallel universe X.

Champions project enthusiasm that not only keeps them fired, but excites those around them.

I could have ignored the stimulus of the spook. But my neurons went berserk and, knowing the PM was in town, I made a connection from seemingly random information.

Champions project enthusiasm that not only keeps them fired, but excites those around them. I was certainly fired up about my magazine, and the chance to interview the Prime Minister – and I like to think this enthusiasm caused the PM to agree to help me fulfil this modest goal.

A champion is an opportunist who will exploit any opportunity to make his dream a reality.

A champion is also an opportunist who will exploit any opportunity to make his dream a reality. I did. My desire to succeed suppressed any fear or embarrassment that would come from a Prime Ministerial rejection.

RON CLARKE

As an athlete he set 19 world track records for distances ranging from two miles to 10 000 metres and was World Sportsman of the Year in 1965 and 1966. He then went on to great success in business and as an author. He is now a champion of philanthropy and President of the CEPA (Council for the Encouragement of Philanthropy in Australia) Trust.

Clarke attributes his own success to the influence of an unsung champion.

LET US FIRST OF ALL ESTABLISH WHAT IS A CHAMPION. IN MY BOOK he, or she, is someone who does extraordinary deeds with the talents and resources they have available. In Australia we tend to only classify our sporting heroes in this way whereas I believe champions can be found in all walks of life.

Allow me to provide just two examples.

I will be accused of outright prejudice but I rate my father, born Thomas Edward Clarke in October 1906, as the equal of any sporting champion that I have ever seen. He was only 12, the eldest of three boys, when his father badly injured his back working on the railway, and he had to become the family provider. So at 14 he started as an apprentice at the Newport workshops, forgoing his dream of entering a profession. Fortunately, he was an

143

outstanding Australian Rules footballer and was able to augment his wages with his earnings from playing with the Essendon Club in the VFL by the time he was 18. In an eight-year career with them he played 148 games, culminating in 1932 when he won the club's Best & Fairest award and represented Victoria. The following year, at the height of the Depression, he switched to the Association to play with Brunswick. This allowed him to put a deposit down on his own house (the VFA paid their stars much more than the VFL did in those days).

Not many footballers or railway workers in the 1930s would have been able to so arrange their affairs so as to purchase a house for a one-income family of four. Dad was described as 'a fast, nuggetty winger with tons of courage and a wet-day specialist', but he was not the superstar my brother Jack became when he played with the Bombers.

As a father, however, he was in a class of his own.

As youngsters, Jack and I waited at the front gate when he was due home so he could join in with our games of football or cricket. There was no greater joy for us than having him kick a ball to us, teaching us how to kick both feet, handball both hands, and pick up the bouncing ball with just the one grab.

But he taught us much more than this. His most precious books were a complete set of the *Encyclopaedia Britannica*, and I would love thinking up sufficiently difficult questions that meant the whole family would troop off to the drawing room and look up the answers. He made a huge counting frame that we learned arithmetic on, letters on cards for us to learn to spell, and exercises to improve and practise our handwriting. As we grew older, evening meals were devoted to debates about a huge range of subjects, from politics to trade unions to sport to religion. I loved these talks.

My father was the most inspiring, most even-tempered, most honest, most friendly man I have ever seen. By example we learned to respect all others, and particularly our opponents on the sporting field; not to take anything for granted just because it had always been done that way; that the most satisfying thing in life is to help others; that earning a living and supporting a family were more important than excelling in sport; and, most importantly, to do whatever task we were undertaking to the best of our ability and with good humour and enthusiasm no matter how menial it may have been.

The point is that champions are not just sportspeople. I would include a large number of men and women I have met in education, in medicine, in scientific research, in business and in all sorts of other activities including, as in the case I have just related, in parenthood.

I'd like to provide another example. Around 18 years ago a very successful businessman, who shall remain nameless, decided he had too much money and set up a philanthropic foundation into which he transferred most of his shareholdings and assets. Since then his foundation has grown so that it now ranks as one of the ten largest in the world. What is unique about it is that all of its gifts are made anonymously. Since 1982 these amount to more than US$2 billion and are currently running in excess of US$500 million per annum.

The man is truly a saint.

In fact, since I have become more involved personally with the non-profit sector of the community through the establishment of our Council for the Encouragement of Philanthropy in Australia I am continually encountering men and women who, in their own right and in their own world, are both heroes and champions.

So what are the ingredients in the makeup of a champion?

I am continually encountering men and women who, in their own right and in their own world, are both heroes and champions ... My champions are invariably modest, respectful of others and an example to all.

First, champions are exceptional. They have undeniable talent mixed with patience, determination, concentration, desire and an insatiable hunger for perfection in their particular vocation. But as well, I believe, they should be outstanding in character and in their contribution to the community to which they belong. So my champions are invariably modest, respectful of others and an example to all, but with a zest for life and people that allows them to completely enjoy doing what they do so well.

SHELLEY TAYLOR-SMITH

Despite suffering terrible back injuries, chronic fatigue syndrome and severe parasitic infections, she set a record in marathon swimming that will never be broken, achieving number one world ranking in what was then a combined men's and women's sport. After this stunning achievement the sport and the prize money were divided along gender lines. Male competitors dubbed her Dangerous When Wet, which is the title of her autobiography.

Mental toughness, she says, made her beat the men at their own game.

IT NEVER OCCURRED TO ME THAT I WOULD BE A MARATHON swimmer. I used to lie in bed and dream, seeing myself like Shane Gould with a gold medal. My hero is Shane Gould. As a little girl I would sit in my beanbag, eating my Rice Bubbles, cheering her on. I know that there are people who actually dreamed that they would succeed in their field. I didn't ever think I'd be a marathon swimmer. As a little girl I did not know there was a sport called marathon swimming.

I used to lie in bed and dream, seeing myself like Shane Gould with a gold medal.

I was not a good swimmer, but I was so keen that I slept with my bathers on. As my mum kissed me good-night she would ask me to put my pyjamas on like a 'normal person', but I had a spare pair tucked inside my pillowcase and would put them on after Mum left my bedroom. I used to wake up seeing myself like Shane Gould and I'd have goosebumps.

For six years I suffered from scoliosis, wearing a steel brace for the duration of high school, but I was determined to swim.

I secured a swimming scholarship at the University of Arkansas. I eventually suffered partial paralysis, spending three months in hospital in traction, and they didn't know if I was ever going to walk again. Consequently I lost my swimming scholarship.

But my coach believed in me. He called me and said: 'In marathon swimming, there are no starts and turns and there is no running either.' All races in marathon swimming start and finish in the water. He said: 'I think you've got what it takes.' I got really excited that somebody believed in me and when my coach told me I had the potential to be a world champion I said, 'What do I have to do?' and he replied, 'Keep swimming.' I knew how to do that!

Here was an opportunity that a lot of people considered a risk. I wasn't even walking that well. But I could swim and I grabbed the opportunity. After many years in a back brace, and in traction, you can understand the freedom I felt in the water. When your body is suspended in water there's no force on your spine.

From 1984 through until 1997 I achieved head-to-head victories against the best men in the sport worldwide, consistently finishing in the top five overall. I am the only woman to ever win a professional marathon swim outright, and became the only woman in professional marathon swimming to hold world race records for both men and women.

I still have the honour of being the only woman in professional marathon swimming to hold the number one world ranking in the sport for both men and women (1991). In 1992, because of my successes and the successes of other women in the sport, the competition was divided into men's and women's competitions with equal prize money, because men were missing out on the higher places and prize money.

People had told me I might never walk again. Someone told me I'd never be good at sport or as a swimmer. I was able to walk again, and I was good at marathon swimming, so why couldn't I beat the men?

One day I heard that Diego Degano, then world champion, had said that if a woman ever beat him he would quit. Two days later I beat him. The satisfaction wasn't necessarily about beating the men, it was about rising to the occasion and going somewhere that nobody else had been before. People had told me I might never walk again. Someone told me I'd never be good at sport or as a swimmer. I was able to walk again, and I was good at marathon swimming, so why couldn't I beat the men? It wasn't about being better than they are; I just loved the challenge.

I think I beat the men because I was mentally tougher. Racing against the men brought out my true potential. If there was anything that my competitors could not take away from me it was my spirit and passion, my desire to be the best I could be and give 100%.

Of course, I loved representing my country – nothing gave me a bigger buzz – but I realised I was representing women around the world. I helped create equal prize money for them. This was a great motivation for me.

In February 1998 I was given six months to live. I was diagnosed as carrying a number of parasites and giardia contracted while swimming in polluted waterways. These various infections had manifested as chronic fatigue syndrome. Doctors told me that if I continued to push myself I was going to die as a result of a complete system failure – organ, circulatory and immune system failure.

Six months later I won the Manhattan Island Marathon Swim for a record fifth time. No other competitor has won the race more than once. I told myself, 'This is as good as it gets' and announced my retirement after representing Australia since 1988.

My motto is: 'If you don't quit, you will make it.'

VISION, DRIVE AND TALENT

A single-minded focus: to be able to concentrate on a task and block out distractions and just go for it.

Shane Gould

To achieve those goals to which one is committed and chooses to dedicate one's life, a belief in yourself is essential.

Nelson Mandela

Analytical intelligence, the capacity to see clearly to the root of a problem, is necessary but not sufficient for a champion in science. Imaginative curiosity, the urgent and creative need to know, is equally important. Finally, the scientist needs drive, the gut-motivated impulse to wrestle the problem to death before someone else does!

Gustav Nossal

Quitters never win. I think hanging in there is tremendously important.

Peter Doherty

DR BRYAN GAENSLER

Young Australian of the Year in 1999 and presenter of the 2001 Australia Day Address, he completed a PhD in Astrophysics, making ground-breaking discoveries relating to the death of stars. He is currently a Hubble Fellow at the Center for Space Research at the Massachusetts Institute of Technology.

But, Gaensler says, many geniuses never become champions.

WHEN PEOPLE TALK TO ME ABOUT THE THINGS I'VE ACCOMPLISHED, they normally conclude with an assertion along the lines of 'You must be so smart to do what you do!'. I wish it were that easy. If being smart was all it took to excel, how come there are so many brilliant people who amount to nothing, and an equal number of people who succeed without being geniuses?

If not sheer brilliance, what does it really take to make a champion in the field of science? For me, there are four watchwords:

- Enthusiasm
- Vision
- Hard work
- Determination

Whenever I doubt myself, whenever I feel that I just can't cut it any more, I remind myself to stay true to these four things.

If you have a spring in your step as you walk into your office, if you have a glint in your eye every time you're explaining what you do, if you have to drag yourself away from your desk because you're caught up in what you're working on, then I believe things will happen.

Let's start with enthusiasm. You have to love what you're doing and believe that it's important. If your heart isn't in it, doors will not open for you. If you have a spring in your step as you walk into your office, if you have a glint in your eye every time you're explaining what you do, if you have to drag yourself away from your desk because you're caught up in what you're working on, then I believe things will happen. Problems will resolve themselves and the job will get done. People will want to work with you, because it's an enjoyable experience to do so.

Working for NASA no doubt sounds wonderful and exciting. Some days it is exciting, but other days are full of administration, printer jams and answering emails.

The second thing you need is vision, because you have to know why you're doing this. You have to have the big picture in mind. Working for NASA no doubt sounds wonderful and exciting. Some days it is exciting, but other days are full of administration, printer jams and answering emails. To maintain your sense of purpose on days like these, you have to have a clear picture in mind of why you're doing it, how the little tasks add up to help you get to where you want to be in ten years' time. It's the difference between just putting one foot in front of the other, and putting energy into dull tasks that need to get done because you know that it's all part of where you want to get to.

Next is determination, because nobody accomplishes anything by giving up. One doesn't have to delve too deeply into the biography of one's heroes to find that before the success and accolades there were apparently insurmountable difficulties and intractable problems that were doggedly overcome. I believe that the only difference between the person standing up on the podium enjoying their success and the one you've never heard of, who never got there, is that one gave up and walked away because they thought they couldn't do it, and the other, even though they felt equally at a loss, was just too pig-headed and determined, and wouldn't give up. By plugging away at the seemingly impossible and by continuing to sink time into a problem, I've been amazed at how I've achieved what I was convinced was impossible.

Short cuts to obscurity, sure. But to success? Unfortunately not.

And finally, and most importantly, the fourth key to my success has been hard work. I often get people telling me that they really are not too keen on putting lots of hours in, and do I know of any short cuts! Short cuts to obscurity, sure. But to success? Unfortunately not.

I find that the best way of convincing people of the value of hard work is to get them to think of the person they most admire, the person that for them defines success, and ask themselves whether this person did what they did through a few easy steps, or whether it took years of dedication, training and practice to make it to the top. Hopefully the answer is pretty obvious — if you want to get anywhere, you have to do the hard yards.

These four mantras capture for me what it takes to be a champion. I hope that by applying them to everything I do, I can continue to achieve.

JOYCE BROWN

Presided over Australia's dominance of international netball, captaining Australian teams to victory in three World Netball Titles. A public speaker on management, teamwork, leadership, communication, ethics and human values in corporate life, education and sport, she is a member of the Sports Hall of Fame and a regular commentator on ABC radio in Melbourne.

Champions, she says, dare to be different.

CHAMPIONS ARE POSITIVE – THERE IS AN INNER DRIVE OF PERSONAL optimism that lifts them beyond the ordinary, beyond what are the established limits to performance, to a service or to the possibilities of solving the mysteries of life.

Champions believe they can. They believe the effort is worth it. They may struggle to find a way, even fail to reach some short-term goals, but their special mindset prevents them being handicapped by self-doubt or negativity. There is an inner expectation to succeed and find a way.

This champion mindset persists – it is passionate in its quest and not always rational. It pushes to get the hard work done to perfect the skills and techniques, so that when the moment is right the mind, heart and body connect – 'the champion connection' is expressed in a peak performance. It happens with the champion singer, musician, dancer, painter, sculptor, scientist and writer – there is an exceptional flow of rhythm, exceptional creativity or understanding. There is an unlocking of possibilities, depth of feeling and expression. In athletic pursuits previous limits are challenged and changed.

Once one person breaks a record, or discovers a cure or a new form of expression, others realise and believe they can now do it, build on it. All dreams become possible when touched by the champion's relentless effort.

The knowledge, physical skill and technique are perfected; then the mindset, the spirit – 'the champion connection' – tackles the previous limits and pushes the performance beyond the normal into what is referred to in athletics as 'the flow' or 'the zone'. It is the performance referred to by an athlete in such terms as 'I had the ball on a string', or 'My feet hardly touched the ground, it all flowed from me'; or in a gruelling 1500 metre race it is the pain registered but overcome by the mind as the physical peak performance is achieved. We know the expression 'She played her heart out'; is that fatuous nonsense, or is it real?

The knowledge, physical skill and technique are perfected; then the mindset, the spirit – 'the champion connection' – tackles the previous limits and pushes the performance beyond the normal into what is referred to in athletics as 'the flow' or 'the zone'.

For the champion, the body, mind and heart (spirit) combine to dare to be different, to take control of the situation with a single-minded dedication to self-belief: 'I can, and I will.'

The joy is being passionately absorbed in that experience for oneself and with others.

DAVID ARMSTRONG

One of the most respected newspaper chiefs in the English-speaking world, he is the long-serving Editor-in-Chief of *The Australian* and past editor of *The Bulletin, The Canberra Times* and Hong Kong's *South China Morning Post.*

Armstrong says that aside from skill and commitment, what makes a champion in any field is a big heart.

RECENTLY, I WAS CHATTING TO A NEWSPAPER PROPRIETOR ABOUT the qualities of a good editor. My view was that the essential quality that made a top editor was the same quality that made a good executive. If we assume we're talking about people with the necessary knowledge, skills and expertise, the factor that lifts the good above the ordinary is commitment. That commitment to the values represented by the newspaper masthead; to free speech and the readers' right to information; to democracy, and the role information and discussion play in it; to the staff; to the readers; and to the town or nation in which the newspaper is published.

Commitment – to oneself, to the endeavour or the team – marks the champion in sport, the arts, politics and business.

Commitment – to oneself, to the endeavour or the team – marks the champion in sport, the arts, politics and business.

But there's one other factor. We talk of champions having big hearts, or strong hearts, as a metaphor for physical ability. A champion also has a big heart emotionally. We talk of loving our champions, but the love fades away if they cannot love too.

AIR COMMODORE JULIE HAMMER

The first woman to command an operational unit in the RAAF and the first woman in the Australian Defence Force to achieve One Star rank. Having joined the Air Force in 1977, she is currently the ADF's Director of General Infrastructure Services.

Here she speaks of the importance of teamwork to a champion.

THE STATUS OF 'CHAMPION' IS ONE THAT IS CONFERRED BY OTHERS. Champions are not self-appointed. They exist only when the achievements of a few are highly valued in the judgement of many. What we value highly varies from decade to decade, from culture to culture. But in general, we have valued as a society through the centuries those feats and achievements that are widely regarded as very difficult either intellectually or physically. We value those feats and achievements that we believe we could not succeed in ourselves. We value as champions those who are judged to be the best at what they do.

In general, to confer the status of 'champion' on a person, we must regard what they do as being worthwhile. It must be enlightening, entertaining, educational, challenging, ground-breaking or beneficial to humanity. Feats outside those categories tend to be 'curiosities' rather than achievements, more suited to an entry in the *Guinness Book of Records*.

There are, arguably, two categories of champions: those who excel through their own individual feats and achievements and those who excel through leading and inspiring team feats and achievements. Are there common attributes that these champions share? Are there key differences between them? What are the characteristics and skills essential to each type of champion? What captures the eye of the beholder?

Determination

Individual achievement, whether intellectual or physical, requires enormous dedication and determination. Some natural talent is essential, but it can only achieve so much. Hard work is the key success factor in any individual or team achievement. No success is ever achieved without hard work and this requires absolute determination to succeed and commitment to success.

> *High achievers believe in themselves. They have faith in their own capabilities. Their goals and aspirations grow as their capability grows. They are optimists.*

Optimism

High achievers believe in themselves. They have faith in their own capabilities. Their goals and aspirations grow as their capability grows. They are optimists. Champions set themselves goals that they believe are just beyond what they can achieve, and when they achieve them, they set new goals higher again. Their belief in themselves and in the goals to which they aspire is unwavering. They believe, ultimately, nothing is out of reach.

Energy

Whatever the achievement for which a champion is recognised, an essential part of a champion's character is abundant stamina and high levels of energy. Champions of any physical pursuit must be fit, healthy and bursting with energy but this tends to be true of intellectual champions too. We all wonder how they cram so much into every day. Normally, high levels of energy can be sustained only through good health. A sensible diet and exercise routine is as important to an intellectual champion as it is to an athletic champion. This high energy appears to come naturally, but in truth it requires enormous lifestyle commitment.

Teamwork

Finally, no champion can achieve through solely their own efforts. Racing-car drivers have support crews, athletes have coaches, musicians have teachers, and most champions have a network of family and friends. Individual achievement derives from that team support. However, in the case of a champion team, while team success derives from individual achievement, it also derives from much more. A champion team can achieve far more than the sum of the individual achievements of its members. The team itself creates energy and enthusiasm. It inspires itself and, unlike an individual champion, the members of a champion team must focus on each other and not just themselves. They must be highly collaborative and supportive, always believing that the team can win.

> *A champion team can achieve far more than the sum of the individual achievements of its members.*

However, it is in the qualities of leadership that lie the key differences between champions who achieve as individuals and champions who achieve through leading teams. Team leader champions must be just as much team members as they are team leaders. Moreover, they must exhibit in abundance the leadership characteristics of fairness, honesty, reliability and strength. They must set the example, make the hard decisions, and create the vision for the team. Then finally, they must inspire the team to reach that vision. Few teams will succeed without a champion to provide that leadership.

What then makes a champion? In the eye of the beholder, champions are those who are judged to be the best at what they do. They become the best through absolute determination and commitment to their goals. These they pursue with boundless energy, continuously raising their goals higher. They believe in themselves and their team and are able to inspire others through their achievements. They are those few who have reached the heights to which the rest of us aspire.

SUSIE MARONEY

The first athlete to swim from Cuba to the United States, she then completed the longest recorded swim in human history: from Mexico to Cuba. Asthmatic and an ordinary swimmer as a child, she was determined to make her mark on the sport.

Maroney's champions are those who overcome what some might consider insurmountable adversities.

A CHAMPION IS NOT NECESSARILY SOMEONE WHO COMES FIRST, but rather someone who has put 100% into whatever goal they set out to achieve. If a child comes sixth in his class in the weekly Maths test having put everything into studying and preparing for it then in my mind that child is a champion.

Monica Seles made a comeback to tennis after being stabbed and is still not in the top five but she is still, in my view, a champion.

But what makes a champion?

When identical twins reach an elite level in sport they seem to be almost identical in talent, but there is always one twin who excels a little bit better than the other. They are the same genetically, so why does one twin beat the other? Same background, same parents, same training.

Sometimes people go through their lives and are never challenged and may never know whether they had the qualities that might have made them stand out from a crowd. Negative parents and disadvantaged surroundings can also contribute to lack of opportunity. Then there are people who rise above all these negatives and become champions in spite of adversity. They strive to achieve, to better themselves and to strive for goals just out of their reach.

Sometimes people go through their lives and are never challenged and may never know whether they had the qualities that might have made them stand out from a crowd.

The common denominator in all champions I have met is that there is always a strong role model that made an impression on them as a child. High achievers may be genetically prone to be so, but there is always one person or a turning point that triggered off the part of their mind that willed them to succeed.

I met a German woman in her twenties the day after I first swam the English Channel. I was on the beach in Dover when I saw her being carried over the pebbles by her father. She was being carried because her legs had been amputated above the knees. I learned that she had fallen off her father's tractor on their farm when she was aged four and the tractor had rolled over the legs. She spent many years in and out of hospital and vowed to set herself a challenge so that if she succeeded she would know she could then do anything she wanted for the rest of her life. She chose to set herself the goal of swimming the English Channel. That first year she didn't make it. But she returned the following year and was successful after 19 hours in the water.

High achievers may be genetically prone to be so, but there is always one person or a turning point that triggered off the part of their mind that willed them to succeed.

That really made an impression on me and I thought that I could perhaps reach higher and set more goals, so I also returned to Dover and went on to swim a double crossing and then on to the Caribbean swims.

I think that champions or super-achievers are ordinary people. They become extraordinary by – what I read years ago – cultivating what the German writer Goethe called 'the genius, power and magic' that exists in all of us.

HARRY M. MILLER

Australia's most recognised entrepreneur in show business and marketing. His theatrical triumphs include *The Rocky Horror Show* and *Hair*. He has created the biggest celebrity management business in Australia.

Harry says we can all be champions but that we move forward together or not at all.

EVERY HUMAN BEING IS EXTRAORDINARY. EVERY PERSON ON THIS planet has something important to say and do. No matter how small your contribution may seem, there is a place set aside for you in the pantheon of champions.

The word 'champion' is synonymous with excellence. Whether it be at the Olympics, in business or in the arts, we salute champions as those individuals who, as a result of special gifts and extraordinary application, stand out for their achievements, resetting the standards by which we measure ourselves. Champions are those individuals at the top of their chosen field, the absolute best. They are 'winners'.

And this is the problem.

To define champions as winners implies that everyone else is a loser. It seems it is human nature to seek and applaud the individual who achieves victory by defeating the many. The vernacular of success constantly reinforces this attitude of 'beating the competition'.

I celebrate excellence by an individual in virtually every field of endeavour. But I believe that a true champion is someone who elevates themselves to a higher level and who takes others along with them.

This is the sort of champion we need today. People like Nelson Mandela. People who care and act about reconciliation in this country. People like the champions at the Salvation Army and contemporary thinkers like High Court Justice Michael Kirby.

We have arrived at a point in time where the divisions between the extremes of excess and insufficiency have never been greater. Half the planet glitters brightly with spectacular inventions and a cornucopia of delights. The less fortunate half, however, struggles to maintain even the most basic quality of life and their future is decidedly bleak. The world can seem a cruel place. Nature does not play favourites: homes and livelihoods can be swept away in an instant; death and disease claim young and old alike.

There has never been a greater need for true champions.

It may seem strange to those who are enjoying good health and good fortune that these are dark days for the human race. Wealth is no substitute for poverty of the human spirit, and as a global society we are running on empty. Countries are torn apart by greed, violence, disease, famine, political chaos and ignorance; ignorance that breeds disease and hate with equally dramatic results – ignorance that feeds the beast of war with the mantra, 'What I do not understand I must fear and what I fear I must destroy.'

Have you ever stopped to consider how many fewer weapons of mass destruction there would be if we focused on a new understanding: learning about our fears and the differences that encourage them? Our goal should not be to destroy our enemies but to make them our friends. When I mentioned this point to Bradley Trevor Grieve, best-selling author of *The Blue Day Book*, he noted with some irony that the essence of what I am saying is the motto of the Australian Army's elite parachute training school – 'Knowledge Dispels Fear'.

There has never been a greater need for true champions. Potential champions are people like you and me, basic people who can change the world. We can rise to the challenge, we can elevate ourselves as human beings to enjoy a life that is more than mere survival. It may seem a daunting task to most and an impossible task to many, but I recently read that a scientist had fired a laser into cesium gas and had successfully sent out a symphony, notated with subatomic particles, faster than the speed of light – just another example of the impossible becoming possible.

The ordinary person can be a true champion by achieving the extraordinary. And what seems extraordinary to most will seem very ordinary to anyone who chooses to realise their full potential, to look into themselves and grasp the bright light inside their heart and hold it up for all the world to see. We are all capable of so much, yet we achieve so little. The last time I checked there were no fewer hours in the day now than when Edison, Curie, da Vinci and Picasso walked the earth.

We can all be true champions if we commit to achieving victory for the many. To do this we only need courage to acknowledge our weaknesses and to do whatever we can to overcome them. In truth, the only real battles worth waging in this world are internal, inside our own hearts. And we must daily take to this battlefield as if our lives and the lives of all we hold dear depend on our victory – for indeed they do.

When we have real courage we will not be held back by ignorance. We will then be able to embrace our place amongst the many, not just tolerating but completely embracing the many differences between ourselves and others, and be able to seek out the great victory without the great glory. Like a true champion.

I firmly believe that our purpose on this planet is to contribute, in every way possible, to the strength and beauty of the human spirit. We move forward together or not at all. This objective and ultimate victory transcends human endeavour and achievement that, like all man-made things, will eventually fade and fall from view.

You may think that you have nothing worth giving, that you have nothing remarkable to contribute, that you are insignificant to the big picture. This would be a tragic mistake.

A true champion is someone who thinks beyond self-interest and who has committed all that they have for the betterment of others. You may think that you have nothing worth giving, that you have nothing remarkable to contribute, that you are insignificant to the big picture. This would be a tragic mistake.

I would like you to imagine a tiny drop of water in

the palm of your hand. It is so small that it seems use-less. If you let it spill onto the street it will soon vanish in the heat. It is not enough to wash your face or quench your thirst. It is not enough to bring life to a freshly planted seed. It is not enough to brush your teeth with. But if you take that tiny drop of water, walk down to the beach and pour it into the sea, it immediately ceases to be a useless little drop of water – for it has now become part of the great ocean itself.

MARK BETHWAITE

A world champion sailor, he is also a high achiever in the corporate sector, having worked as a resources adviser to Deutsche Bank and many of Australia's top mining companies. He is currently Chief Executive of Australian Business Limited, an industry lobby group.

Mark started out wanting to win Olympic gold in one class of sailing, but finished up world champion of another.

WHAT IS IT THAT DRIVES CHAMPIONS — IS IT INNATE, OR IS IT learned? How does a champion identify a goal worthy of their talents?

I thought that I had some natural talent in sailing. In the early days of my sailing I saw a Flying Dutchman class yacht and was told it was an Olympic class. From that time on my sole aim was to win an Olympic gold medal in that class. That goal I never achieved, but my crew and I became world champions in another Olympic class, the Soling, immediately after the 1980 Olympic sailing events.

My formula for success, particularly when leading teams, is:

- Realistic goal setting
- Commitment by all team members

- Preparation that results in legitimate confidence by all team members
- Making it happen: resolve and calculated risk-taking are essential elements in successful execution.

This formula has worked for me in business as well as in sailing, and has proved invaluable in turnaround situations, where corporate survival has depended on exceptional team performance.

There is a defining quality about champions that I find compelling – they are passionate about their capacity to make a difference. And champions emerge from all fields of human endeavour. As an example, I am associated with some research scientists who work tirelessly to achieve their goal of a breakthrough in the treatment of cancer. I consider them to be champions.

There is a defining quality about champions that I find compelling – they are passionate about their capacity to make a difference.

MICHAEL RENNIE

A promising future lay before this Rhodes Scholar. Diagnosed with cancer, however, he nearly died at the age of 30. Twelve years later he is a father of two and a director of one of the world's most powerful management consultancies, McKinsey & Co.

Rennie offers his insights into dealing with adversity and suggests the key elements of a corporate champion.

CHAMPIONSHIP REQUIRES A COMBINATION OF BOTH WILL AND skill. One will not do – both are always in evidence in championship.

This, of course, raises two questions:

1. Where does the will come from? In other words, what drives business champions?
2. What capabilities or skills do champions in business exhibit?

In my experience with champions in business, every person's source of drive is unique. No two business leaders are exactly the same. Yet it seems that, being human, we are 'hard-wired' with certain drives.

Each person's drive is a unique (and over time, changing) fingerprint. If I sought to draw a map of this territory I would start with Maslow's hierarchy of needs. Simplified, these are:

1. Physiological or survival needs – shelter, safety, food and procreation.
2. Belonging needs – love, tribal community and belonging.
3. Achievement needs – self-esteem and achievement.
4. Self-actualisation needs – this begins with self-awareness and a relationship with inner self. It grows in relationships with others, making a difference, being of service, and spirituality.

We operate on all these levels at once. Yet, for each of us, the centre of gravity of our personality is unique, giving our fingerprint. It also changes with time. Maslow would say that for successful people the centre of gravity of personality moves from survival through belonging and achievement to self-actualisation.

A big part of the journey for me has been to become increasingly aware of what really drives me at a deeper level. I have found that if I shift my inner world, my external world shifts. I think of it as leadership or championship from the inside.

I often ask myself what it is that really drives me. What is my 'fingerprint'? I have found that there is a trick in this question. My will is both conscious and subconscious. Carl Jung described the conscious mind as a cork floating on the ocean of the subconscious. Much of my will is the product of mindsets, beliefs and stories that I am not consciously aware of. A big part of the journey for me has been to become increasingly aware of what really drives me at a deeper level. I have found that if I shift my inner world, my external world shifts. I think of it as leadership or championship from the inside.

The champions I know in business are driven by a combination of fear and love.

Often I see fear as a driver – fear of not paying the rent (survival), fear of not being respected and accepted (love and belonging), fear of failure (self-esteem). Love, on the other hand, is not a word we use in business (yet), but being driven by love is to be driven by the desire to grow, to see others grow, to be of service, to have fun and enjoy, to work in a trusting and respectful environment that is meaningful.

The champions I know in business are driven by a combination of fear and love. Business champions also achieve their results by working through others. They lead others through fear and love. There is something remarkable happening in the business environment throughout the Western world. We are witnessing a shift away from fear in championship.

The globalisation of markets and the transparency of financial results in capital markets has created an extraordinary pressure to perform, and we know that fear and hierarchy can get us some of the way towards this. However, we also know that the information revolution has created the need for everyone throughout the whole company to be pursuing our goals of innovation and change continuously. I can no longer tell everyone what to do; rather, I need to create an environment with a clear vision and agreed values and allow people to act with much more trust within that. Hence we are creating what we might call co-creative enterprises. This transition is the great challenge and opportunity that business championship faces today.

Now to skill. We are finding that championship in business is truly multi-dimensional. As human beings we live and experience in four ways simultaneously: the physical (doing), the mental (ideas), the emotional (feelings) and the spiritual (meaning).

Champions in business require all four. In fact we are finding that they require more emotional and spiritual resources than had previously been thought.

> *We are hard-wired for meaning. Where people are doing something that has meaning, there is greater drive and energy. Champions in business see meaning in what they do and are able to help others connect the task at hand to their meaning.*

Physically, they require stamina and the ability to physically release stress. Mentally, they need to be smart (IQ). They need to have knowledge of the business area. Interestingly, however, we are learning that emotional strength helps more. This is what is now being called EQ (emotional quotient). It has been found to be more important to business success than IQ. Emotional intelligence is the ability to connect with my own emotions and those of others and to work with these productively. Spiritual needs are about meaning. We are hard-wired for meaning. Where people are doing something that has meaning, there is greater drive and energy. Champions in business see meaning in what they do and are able to help others connect the task at hand to their meaning.

Who are the true champions? I often wonder whether the people we see written about in the press (because they are the best at something) are the only true champions. We know that becoming the best at one thing most often requires the sacrifice of other aspects of our lives. Many business champions feel an imbalance in their lives. They crave time for relationships, for family, and for their own quiet time. I know very talented people who have chosen not to be the best at one thing, but to be the best at living a full life, to know themselves well enough to know how much time and mindspace to commit to each of the areas of their lives – to business, to community, to family, to friends, and to self.

Irene Claremont de Castillejo has captured it for me when she says:

> Only a few achieve the colossal task of holding together, without being split asunder, the clarity of their vision alongside an ability to take their place in a materialistic world. These are the modern heroes. Artists at least have a form within which they can hold their own conflicting opposites together, but there are some who have no recognised artistic form to serve this purpose. They are the artists of the living. To my mind, these last are the supreme heroes in our soulless society.

These people are the champions of living. We don't celebrate them. In the future, we will more.

One of my biggest lessons has been about joy and

burden in championship. I have a friend who is a businessman who always wanted to make a film. It was a great unrealised passion. He is an extraordinary man and he has made the film. Halfway through, he began to find it a burden. The joy went out of it. He was very concerned about it being successful. He carried that concern and it burdened him. We all know that feeling. The joy returned when he let go of the outcome. He just turned up each day and gave it his very best. The film would be what it would be. This has been a huge lesson for me. It is what is often called in the world of philosophy 'non-attachment'. It doesn't mean that you don't focus totally on the result. On the contrary, you hold a strong vision of success but you also know that it will be what it will be. You give the task your all without fear. In fact because you have no fear or concern, you are stronger, better, and your light shines brighter.

The joy returned when he let go of the outcome. He just turned up each day and gave it his very best.

DI MORRISSEY

One of Australia's best-selling authors. Her novels address matters that go deep into the Australian psyche, including issues of reconciliation, environment, gender and ageism. Morrissey is a spokesperson for the National Breast Cancer Centre and the Royal Flying Doctor Service.

Here she reflects on the circumstances that led to her career as an author.

WHAT MAKES A CHAMPION? HAS MADE ME ATTEMPT TO IDENTIFY the combination of factors that over decades enabled me to reach a high level of achievement. The reflection and careful assembly of the events, people, and places led to the identification of so much that clearly had an impact, yet had, until now, been overlooked.

I found it necessary to make an objective list of the factors and influences that make a champion in any field.

There are personal factors: innate ability, attitude, self-motivation and discipline, tenacity and dedication, adaptability and flexibility, sacrifice and courage.

Then there are environmental factors: influences, opportunity (access to training, education and facilities), challenges at home and in the community, encouragement, support and understanding (from family, friends, teachers, employers, community, heroes and mentors).

With those guidelines I looked back and now put fresh value on a great many steps in my journey to where I am today.

My early years were spent with my grandparents in a country town in New South Wales as my mother was working in Sydney. My grandfather was a railway worker, but before migrating to Australia he was a 'scholarship boy' in London and loved reading. When he married and set up house in the town, one of his early acquisitions was a bookcase with leadlight doors. I was encouraged to explore its shelves before I could read. My grandparents read book after book, and reading to me simply became a happy and treasured time with a book. The environment encouraged the imagination. Later I too became a voracious reader.

I had the freedom to roam the bush with my young uncles, to explore, to observe nature, to invent wild adventure games, with one rule – to be home before dark.

There was always time in those days for the grown-ups to sit about yarning. And they never seemed to mind me listening in. They joked and argued, sang and played harmonicas and squeezeboxes, sat around fires in the winter, and in the moonlight on the lawns in the summer.

There was the mystery machine my grandfather (Poppy) kept on a high shelf in the kitchen. It took a little while for me to learn that the ancient cumbersome manual typewriter was connected to the business of words. Poppy wrote frequent reports for the local newspaper. The ritual of setting up the machine and the careful composition of a 'story' fascinated me. I was allowed to play with the keyboard, but the actual telling of my stories had to find another outlet. I found it in my backyard chook-pen. No-one was the least perturbed at my penchant for hypnotising a red rooster or white leghorn hen and taking them to bed to tell them my stories.

Later I would peck out stories on Poppy's typewriter (now in the Wingham museum), aware that this was a meaningful and respected pastime.

At six my mother and the man I regarded as my father moved to Pittwater, an isolated community outside Sydney accessible only by boat. The national park was my backyard and I enjoyed more freedom than even a country town offered. Sharing the isolated bush-fringed bays were a cultured and eccentric mob: Mary Stackhouse, mother of two journalists, who guided my reading, travel writer George Farwell, composer George English, poet Dorothea Mackellar, and actor Chris Rafferty. Their doors were always open. Books, writing, and performing were part of everyday life.

Dorothea Mackellar was a patient listener to the stories I invented about the bush. She said: 'That is quite splendid. But one day you must write them down so others can enjoy them.' It was the first time anyone had suggested a link between my telling stories and writing them.

Then tragedy struck. My father and baby brother drowned. Mum and I went to America to stay with her sister in California as part of the grieving and recovery process. I was exposed to Hollywood and the American dream, and the miracle of television, which my mother began to study at college in San Francisco. This led her to a career in the newly launched Australian TV industry, becoming our first woman commercial TV director.

While she built a career, I was more or less lost, as a neophyte photographic model and actress, until another influence got me back on the storytelling trail. My uncle Jim Revitt, also inspired by the old typewriter and lead-light library, returned from a long overseas stint as a journalist. He guided me into the bowels of the Sydney *Telegraph* to meet a subeditor, Mac Jeffers, who became a mentor to me through a journalism cadetship.

This led to a period in London's Fleet Street as a women's editor. Returning home I detoured to Malaysia, met and married an American diplomat, spending several years in several countries as a diplomatic wife and mother, unsuspectingly building up experiences and collecting characters that one day would populate my books.

I continued to write for newspapers and magazines, worked for an international advertising agency and got into television, hosting my own show and producing for the American CBS network.

And then one morning I woke up and wondered whatever had happened to the dream of that young girl. And those environmental factors shouted: 'Go – do it.' Somehow I found the courage to listen and act. I walked away from a marriage and a high-profile television career in Sydney to a hideaway, relative poverty, and the loneliness of the creative writer facing a fresh blank page, day after day.

One morning I woke up and wondered whatever had happened to the dream of that young girl.

Now was the time for tenacity, dedication. I didn't know the cost it would carry – the separation, the deprivation, the risks, the knocks, the battles and the struggles. But the reward – to one day hold that book of my stories knowing other people did enjoy them – was worth it.

My children tell me I've set them an example of survival, of achievement, of never giving up. Along with all the championship attributes already mentioned, I can add one more piece of advice, and that is to follow my grandfather's advice: 'Shoulders back, chin up, and put one foot in front of the other.'

CAN ANYBODY BE
A CHAMPION?

Most people are born with talent but the majority of people don't know about their talent.

Gennadi Touretski

The trick is to really identify what our gift is.

Di Morrissey

A champion is someone who is willing to stand apart from the crowd in order to achieve his or her chosen goal. This can often mean isolation and loneliness ... Achieving the goal is almost secondary to the mental and physical discipline and strength required to make the decision to go for that goal.

Anne Summers

The common feature possessed by all those whom I admire is ... A willingness to be confident outside the tribe. For this to be translated into achievement a degree of sheer bloody-mindedness is essential.

Gavin Brown

PHILLIP ADAMS

Journalist, broadcaster, author and commentator, he is the father of the modern Australian film industry and the National Institute for Dramatic Art. Phillip has left an indelible imprint on the way we interpret Australian identity.

Champions are inevitable, he says, but the boundaries of human achievement will continue to expand as we reduce barriers to participation.

WHAT MAKES A CHAMPION? IS IT A GIFT FROM GOD? IS IT A genetic endowment that's pre-ordained, as is a propensity for cardiac disease? Or, talking of matters cardiovascular, is it a consequence of having a great heart? If not in the sense of Phar Lap's, hugely magnified in its jar of formaldehyde, then perhaps in the metaphoric sense? Or is championship driven from something in the spirit, from somewhere in the vast constellation of neurons and synapses that seethe and spark within the skull? If it isn't nature then is it perhaps nurture? Is it the stage mother pushing the child towards stardom? Is it having an obsessive dad who insists that 'You, young man, will become Wolfgang Amadeus Mozart', or 'You, young James Packer, will take over as the richest man in Australia'?

I've entertained the possibility in a recent essay that

the champion is, in a sense, a statistical inevitability. Someone has to be the richest man in Australia. It's like being the tallest man or the fattest man or the oldest woman. The pressure of a population of 20 million, let alone 200 million, is that spectacularly endowed individuals have to emerge from the pressure of numbers. A bit like diamonds emerging from the pressures applied to common or garden carbon. Mind you, the individuals that sometimes emerge as world champions may not be as spectacular as you might hope. Look at the immense lack of enthusiasm among American voters as they move reluctantly towards polling day, so vastly unenthusiastic about the contenders that a majority do not even bother voting.

> *I've entertained the possibility in a recent essay that the champion is, in a sense, a statistical inevitability.*

In the case of the US elections, the pressure of population and of prejudice eliminates a huge number of people with the potential to be champions; to be great presidents. For a start, you eliminate 50% of the population at the outset, before you even start thinking about policies or issues, simply because they're women. You have to eliminate, at least for the time being, the African Americans from contention, as Colin Powell knows very well; as Jesse Jackson knew better. White America is not yet ready, it would seem, for a black president. And for similar reasons they eliminate Hispanic Americans, and until a second ago it was widely believed that you had to eliminate Jews. Three cheers to Gore for breaking that taboo.

Less contentiously, you have to eliminate those who are too young to be credible, or those deemed too old for the task, although Reagan of course pushed that envelope. And in the US, despite it being a nation of immigrants, despite the symbolism of the Statue of Liberty, you eliminate immigrants. So that, for example, a Henry Kissinger could have a career in the White House, be all too familiar with the Oval Office, but never be president. You have to eliminate those with a criminal record, although all too often criminals have been within a heartbeat of the world's highest office – look at Spiro Agnew.

This process also involves getting rid of people who are insufficiently telegenic, and it means you finish up with your choice of Bush or Gore. Now the Prime Minister and I disagree on whether or not we should have a president, but we wholeheartedly agree on the inadmissibility of having one who is directly elected, because I think that American process would come into play and we won't get a Bill Deane out of it. Is the most powerful person in the world, an American President, a champion? He often gets the job through misadventure or happenstance. Harry Truman was a pretty good president but he was in no way a champion, having failed as an oil prospector and in various business ventures – he wasn't even a good haberdasher. But he got the job because Roosevelt died in office. And then there are those who got the job through assassination.

But whether you're talking about athletics or science or politics or the arts, whether championship is written in the stars or comes in effect in a flash of lightning, I can think of no more fascinating subject to research, to discuss and to enjoy. And we hope that the contributions of the many champions involved in this discussion will add up to, not a T.O.E. – a Theory of Everything – but a theory perhaps of excellence. And perhaps Allan Snyder will be able to write an equation that will be as simple and exhilarating as Einstein's $E=MC^2$.

I should make the point that in athletics the issue of championship seems so much simpler, so pure and unarguable. But there are new arguments too about the dazzling performances we've seen at contests like the Olympics. One of the reasons for the faster times and higher jumps lies not merely in sports medicine or new training techniques and, thank God, not in drugs, but in the fact that now things are changing. Now millions who were denied the opportunity to participate in this or that sport are, albeit reluctantly, being included.

One of the reasons for the faster times and higher jumps lies not merely in sports medicine or new training techniques and, thank God, not in drugs, but in the fact that now things are changing. Now millions who were denied the opportunity to participate in this or that sport are, albeit reluctantly, being included.

Tiger Woods comes to mind because golf, like baseball before it, was a closed world to African Americans. Suddenly, across America black kids are playing golf and those white golf clubs are being forced to admit them. And similarly we're about to see an explosion of black talent in Mandela's South Africa as organisations like the South African Cricket Board are forced to allow blacks to don cricket whites.

So by adding to the talent pool all over the world we're making possible the emergence of new champions.

PRIME MINISTER JOHN HOWARD

Prime Minister of Australia 1996–2007. He is the quintessential political champion, having overcome many years of political adversity to emerge triumphant in the long haul.

He says that a champion can see the present as the foundation from which any future can be built.

THERE ARE CHAMPIONS IN EVERY FIELD OF HUMAN ENDEAVOUR — champions in areas of physical endurance and achievement, champions of the mind, champions of the human spirit. All of them combine the attributes of excellence, endurance, character and courage to redefine the accepted limits of human insight and accomplishment.

And yet so little is understood about that intangible force of nature that continues to elevate mankind to new heights. Will some individuals succeed no matter what the circumstances of their birth or upbringing or education? Does the defining life-force of a champion, like running water, create its own channels regardless of the barriers placed before it? Can excellence be taught, mentored or encouraged?

These questions are complex and intriguing. What is known is that champions enrich the lives of all of us.

They view the world as full of possibilities, not problems. They see the present, not as an inevitable consequence of the past, but as a foundation on which any future can be built. They prove to all of us that one person with courage, imbued with a sense of what is right and what is just, accepting personal responsibility for their own future – and, most importantly, that of others – can make a difference.

What is known is that champions enrich the lives of all of us. They view the world as full of possibilities, not problems.

Australia is a nation of champions. It is no secret that I, along with most other Australians, delight in the successes of Australian sportsmen and women. Yet I am equally proud that our nation produced some of the most extraordinary people of the 20th century – people who have been champions of science and medicine, of international relations and humanitarian aid, and champions of freedom and democracy itself.

I have every confidence that Australia will continue to produce ever more champions in every field of endeavour.

BAZ LUHRMANN

Director and producer. Propelled into the spotlight by *Strictly Ballroom*, his most recent sensation is *Moulin Rouge*. Luhrmann draws together a diverse set of skills from stage, musical theatre, opera, film and pop music, creating a new genre.

A CHAMPION IS NO LESS FALLIBLE THAN ALL OF US, YET THEIR deeds and achievements stand as a sign. It is all these signs and symbols that we look to when as human beings we feel lost. It is for this reason that we need champions.

SHANE GOULD

Became the darling of a nation after winning five Olympic medals at the 1972 Olympic Games at the age of 15. In September 1972 she held every women's freestyle world record from 100 metres to 1500 metres. She then retired from swimming under the pressure of celebrity aged 16. Her re-emergence as a public figure in the lead-up to the 2000 Games demonstrated that after more than 20 years of seclusion she was still adored by the nation.

Here Gould talks about the champion and her relationship with her audience.

A CHAMPION NEEDS A SOCIAL CONTEXT TO BEAR THE LABEL OF champion. To be acknowledged as a champion, they need validation by the judgements of others.

A person sails single-handed around the world. She tells no-one of her intention. She arrives safely at the end of her journey and quietly goes home without any welcoming crowd. Her effort is of epic proportion, but no-one knows what she has done.

A woman sits in meditation in a snow cave for years, enduring extraordinary privation in a search for enlightenment. No-one from her own society knows what she has been doing.

In both of these cases the person must tell others, possibly by writing a book, before her society can give her the epithet of champion.

It is rare and inappropriate in our culture for someone to call themselves a champion; it is more usual for the term to be accorded by popular consent – often by the media initiating the term. Here is the most seductive and distracting point in a champion's life. A champion has some sort of personal quest that they achieve but, once it becomes public, needs to learn to deal with a public audience – one that often pries into personal and private realms quite apart from their area of championship – and continue on with their quest.

Our culture suffers from championitis. The consumption of heroes is like psychological fast food, un-nourishing and a slow and deadly poison.

In order for the champion to arouse more than just people's enthusiasm she has to be self-disciplined and humble to stay focused on her quest and do something more than be a star.

Here is the paradox. For a champion to be a champion they need an audience. But when a private identity becomes a 'public image' it devalues inner life and character. When saints become 'stars' the process devalues models of spiritual growth. When followers become 'fans' the process devalues discipleship. When the gifted become 'glamorous' the process devalues leadership and spiritual authority. When wisdom, understanding and experience become 'endorsements, personal glimpses and slogans' the process devalues faith.

In order for the champion to arouse more than just people's enthusiasm she has to be self-disciplined and humble to stay focused on her quest and do something more than be a star.

To be a champion one has to live in such a way that others can have a better life. A champion's actions and deeds have to cause change in the way others think and act. They then become leaders, and remain gifted, sharing their wisdom and understanding from their experience.

.

SIMON TEDESCHI

Prodigy and musical genius. He first performed a Mozart piano concerto at the Sydney Opera House aged nine. His perform-ances internationally have attracted critical acclaim. But as a child it was suggested that he was developmentally disabled.

Tedeschi's account of a moment on the sporting field reveals the importance of being able to look a fool for a greater cause.

CHARLIE PARKER WAS ONCE ASKED HOW HE PLAYED THE WAY HE DID. He replied: 'Well, you gotta learn all your scales and chords, keep your fingers in good shape, listen to lots of great people and keep your mind sharp. Then, once you've done all that, forget that crap and just play.' Well, I think he was and is right, but that's another challenge for me.

My parents observed early on in my life that if I wasn't good at something, they were going to have to take drastic action. It was even suggested that I may have been developmentally disabled, for at the age of four I was incredibly small and almost backward, with an uncanny tendency to stare aimlessly at the wall. A void in my life would have to be filled, or else!

My love of music is a great compromise where the music usually wins.

From the outset, I was told I had a great aptitude for piano – naturally my family were thrilled, perhaps out of relief more than anything. And then my life was split in two, as so often happens – my life before the piano, and my life during. Like any marriage, my love of music is a great compromise where the music usually wins. This is the first obstacle I had to bear in the quest to be a champion. Because music is so volatile and is entirely subject to an almost infinite number of variables, I learned early on that my career (and I had already decided upon such things at age six) would be subject to extreme highs and lows. I believe it's called artistic temperament.

When I was ten, I was playing cricket with my primary school team, suffering from the delusion that I was a talented bowler, batsman, fielder and all-round cricketing genius. I was fielding on the boundary (which is where they always put me) and the batsman hit a 'skier', which means he hit a ball a couple of hundred metres into the air, killing a few stray north-shore pigeons in the process. The ball was coming in my direction, and I had to make a decision that has since stayed with me through every day of my life – do I catch the ball and possibly injure my hands, or let it drop to the ground and lose my dignity? Of course, I chose the latter, resulting in our opponents' resounding victory and a barrage of abuse from my 'mates', who were by now expressing their discomfort by throwing furniture. But this story is not an isolated incident – by entering this undoubtedly fruitful and rewarding life, you must first work out your priorities. Sometimes, even the most rudimentary of tasks is a risk. That is not to say I wear rubber gloves in supermarkets. It simply means that such activities as karate, chopping (in the kitchen), gardening, and quite a few sports are definite no-nos for me. Some people think I am overreacting – Horowitz was known to use large garden saws without any hesitation or protection. That's fine for you, Vladimir, but I don't think I could do that, mainly because of the immense part music plays in my life and my family's.

I have no hesitation in mentioning that my ego is bigger than the outdoors. But it has been a cultivated one, not a natural one. If I have children, and the Lord knows I have a great many years left to create more egoists, I don't think I would recommend the life of a musician. It's rewarding, but oh so tough. I spend roughly ten months touring, away from everyone and everything dear to me. I have seen more hotel rooms than most people I know, and even 'appropriating' the bathroom supplies has become uninteresting. I have encountered so many people – lovely ones, strange ones (pianists take note here), stars, taxi drivers, the list goes on. And when this happens to you when you are a child – the last I checked, I am still one of those – two things happen: you begin to talk predominantly like and with adults, and you 'toughen up', hence ego. Being asked to write 1000 words on my favourite subject is like a red rag to a bull!

> *I have no hesitation in mentioning that my ego is bigger than the outdoors.*

There is no doubt in my mind that no matter how much talent you have, or how good your chops are, in this business you have to work at it. And let's face it, nothing's quite as bad as a Czerny study or a Hanon finger exercise; I personally prefer to stare at a wall. But you gotta do it, I've found that out the hard way. Music is the most tiresome and the most beautiful job in the world, and I wouldn't swap it for anything – except a little less practice and Czerny studies. Sometimes I wonder what type of man would devote his life to writing music that sounds like fairy floss.

> *Have I mentioned love, joy, festivity, spirituality, friendship, learning, growing, admiring, communicating?*

What makes a champion? Maybe compromise, ego, work and denial? Have I mentioned love, joy, festivity, spirituality, friendship, learning, growing, admiring, communicating? No, but that should be obvious. If any of you ever see me on stage I am quite often seen with a goofy smile. I am, quite simply, enjoying myself, because my home is the stage. What makes a champion? That question is like 'What is life?' Why on earth would you want to swap an answer for such a beautiful question?

PETER MONTGOMERY

He played no less than 510 internationals with the Australian water polo team, represented Australia in four Olympics, four World Championships and one World Cup.

Foundation President of the World Olympians Association, law practitioner and developer, he says the Olympics are a great 'role model factory'.

IT HAS BEEN SAID: 'NOTHING IN THE WORLD CAN REPLACE PERseverance. Talent cannot – there is nothing more common than misused talent. Genius cannot – geniuses are usually unfulfilled. Education cannot – the world has many educated people with little achievement. Only perseverance and determination are omnipotent.'

An identified ambition followed by years of perseverance are attributes of almost all champions in any field.

One of the greatest benefits of role models in society is their capacity to turn up the light which flickers in the minds of most young people. The role model provides the vehicle for the personal visualisation of the possibility of high achievement by young people in all societies. This mechanism is one of the great benefits of sport – particularly the Olympic Games. It appears to be easier to understand what is needed to become a great sportsman than what is essential to be a great biotechnologist, successful businessman or masterful cinematographer.

It is to the International Olympic Committee's credit that it insists on free-to-air television coverage of all major Olympic events and itself pays to assist television coverage in Africa to ensure its global reach.

Visualisation of the possibility of high achievement is accompanied by the imperceptible realisation that high achievement is not obtained without great and long effort. The Olympic Games is the greatest role model factory in the history of human endeavour.

The less gifted kids develop the greater wish to succeed ... whereas the talented child will often not be prepared to devote himself sufficiently.

It will be interesting to see if goal identification becomes a more difficult task as life becomes more complicated and hurried, and options multiply. Many talented young people can face a difficult decision as to which goal to follow. Many attempt several and usually don't quite make it big in any.

In sport, the most naturally gifted athletes often lack persistence. The less gifted kids develop the greater wish to succeed (and succeed big) whereas the talented child who effortlessly wins everything from a young age will often not be prepared to devote himself sufficiently to proceed to the next level. A number of rugby players who could not make their school's First XV became famous Wallabies (including Wallaby captains).

When on a path towards a high ambition the struggle is a constant one, which is always marked by setbacks and difficulties. The capacity of the person to endure, to never give up the ambition, is, in my opinion, the key factor. Circumstances may frustrate the most determined competitor who possesses all the other qualities but luck. Much rarer is the champion who moves forward effortlessly with no particular goal in mind and then achieves a great triumph.

> *The capacity of the person to endure, to never give up the ambition, is, in my opinion, the key factor.*

The early mental development of a potential champion must be a critical factor. There must be many different parental scenarios which have produced great champions – from fawning to critical, and from encouraging to disparaging.

From my observation, nothing is more certain to result in failure and disappointment to both parties than the parent who is single-mindedly determined that their child will be the great champion the parent hoped to be. There is frequently a crossover point where a wise parent or coach has guided and helped their child towards certain areas of endeavour and the child then takes up the challenge and genuinely aspires to the goal. Whether this aspiration is somehow always linked subconsciously to pleasing a parent or coach (who possibly has long gone from the scene) is not clear.

We have all heard someone vindicate their actions by saying, 'I certainly showed them.' If asked to specify who 'them' is/are, many people would be perplexed by their inability to identify the invisible jury judging their behaviour or performances.

With the increasing amount of activity at a high level in all areas of human endeavour by larger numbers of people, it is gradually getting harder to distinguish a real and unique champion from a person of slightly lesser achievement. It is clear that Tiger Woods is a champion, but what about the other top nine golfers in the world? The average annual round score of the top ten players is now only marginally better than that of the 100th best player.

We marvelled at the skills of some great champions at the 2000 Olympics. Let us hope that they will become role models for an entire generation of potential champions around the world – little girls who want to be like Susie O'Neill and who eventually become prima ballerinas, or little boys who want to copy Ian Thorpe but end up running BHP (or being chancellor of a great university).

PROFESSOR ALLAN SNYDER

Director of the Centre for the Mind. An international award-winning scientist who was named by *The Bulletin/Newsweek* as one of Australia's ten most creative minds. His research spans mind sciences, visual biology, telecommunications, information technology and physics.

His champions are those who fundamentally change the way we think.

MY CHAMPIONS ARE THOSE WHO SHOW US HOW TO SEE THE world differently, especially when this shatters our pre-conceptions. Ghandi, by demonstrating the awesome power of peaceful confrontation; Copernicus with his proof that the earth revolves around the sun; and Roger Bannister in breaking the four-minute mile presumed to have been a physiological barrier.

Champions are ubiquitous. I can not pretend to enumerate the categories or evaluate them in some hierarchical order. Ultimately the process of conferring championship is a highly personal evaluation and one no doubt woven into our dreams and aspirations.

The concept of a champion differs between individuals and even differs in any one individual over time.

Championship is a constantly shifting phenomenon, highly dependent on gender, culture and society.

I have enormous respect for anyone who builds something significant from nothing. That feat requires orchestrating a symphony of diverse talents. You must have attempted the process to even begin to appreciate what I mean.

I also have a special appreciation for the person who links seemingly disparate areas of knowledge, especially when this shows how apparently complex, inexplicable phenomena can be understood from a familiar elementary framework.

But I value the most a person who shows us how to look at the world differently – especially when the process smashes our mindsets and dissolves our preconceptions as did Ghandi, Copernicus and Bannister.

> *But I value the most a person who shows us how to look at the world differently.*

Breaking a mindset is a profoundly important contribution, one that advances civilisation by leaps. It is intrinsically difficult because it requires inventing a new way to look at the world. And it also demands courage to confront conventional wisdom if others are ever to be convinced of its value.

I believe we all have the innate potential to be a champion. The crucial question is: what shapes an individual into performing like one? It is one thing knowing the qualities of a desired champion, but quite another knowing how to educate for these qualities. No doubt there are multiple paths to achieve this goal.

Occasionally the strongest personal characteristics are brought out in defiance of or in opposition to regimes designed to repress these very traits. This is equally true in totalitarian regimes and within oppressive families.

I believe we all have the innate potential to be a champion. The crucial question is: what shapes an individual into performing like one?

It would appear that looking at the world differently requires a mind that enjoys continually reinventing new ways to examine familiar things. A playful mind, one that does not fear mistakes or failures. Someone with a healthy scepticism for authority. Someone who is unafraid of following their intuition. And always someone who has the courage to confront conventional wisdom.

Ultimately, I believe, the process of looking at the world in a completely new way is a celebration of what it means to be human.

DAME
LEONIE KRAMER

One of the most influential Australians. A PhD from Oxford University launched a stunning career including Chancellor of the University of Sydney, Chair of the ABC, Director of St Vincent's Hospital and Commissioner of the New South Wales Electricity Commission.

Here she says champions are driven by passion rather than ambition.

IN DESCRIBING HER EXPERIENCE, SHELLEY TAYLOR-SMITH USES phrases like, 'the best I could be', 'mental toughness', 'to make a lasting contribution', and Shane Gould, 'fitness for life', 'I can do it', 'audacity', 'rejection of fame and stardom', 'the need for competition', 'there's more to life than winning'.

Many sportsmen and women have tried to describe what keeps them going despite all the odds. Their anecdotal evidence about performance bears a strange resemblance to what artists say about the nature of the creative process. They try to describe the feeling that accompanies the genesis of a work, and the compulsion they feel as they set about their task. Some artists have even described this state of mind as a burden imposed from without, or as an irresistible force; and athletes speak of an 'inner voice' which drives them.

One of the reasons why J. K. Rowling's Harry Potter books have been so successful is that Harry embodies many of the qualities we associate with champions. He doesn't seek to be a champion; and he is too modest and intelligent to think of himself as heroic. He is used to battling the odds, confronting criticism and experiencing failure; so he understands that champions do not always win. He is sustained throughout his various trials by his inner voice and his sense of a strong moral imperative, which drive him to challenge the evil forces that threaten the innocent and vulnerable.

Champions are frequently uncomfortable with extravagant praise and are publicity-shy. The constant and repetitious intrusion of some members of the media makes their arduous path to success even harder, because it reaches into their privacy, and touches the core of their self-discipline.

> *Harry Potter embodies many of the qualities we associate with champions. He doesn't think of himself as heroic. He is used to battling the odds, confronting criticism and experiencing failure; so he understands that champions do not always win.*

Surviving defeat and being modest in victory are not necessarily the most conspicuous but are certainly the most valuable qualities of champions.

Champions are driven more by passion for what

they do than by ambition, which explains both their capacity to overcome pain and failure and their reserve when questioned about their feelings.

The idea of championship is still an intriguing mystery – even to those who have had many years to reflect on their victories and defeats.

ALEX HAMILL

Hailed as an advertising guru, his leadership roles include Chair and CEO of George Patterson Bates and Chair of the Communications Group comprising George Patterson Bates, Zenith Media and the Campaign Palace.

His capacity to absorb a complex and diverse set of views and then to distil the cogent message is exemplified here.

HAVING HAD THE CHANCE OF A LIFETIME TO OBSERVE THE MANY who gathered to discuss, debate and analyse what makes a champion, I feel that one quality flows like a mighty river from academic to artist to sportsperson to business leader to politician.

While it would seem ridiculous to suggest that these great leaders had only this quality to attribute their success to, the fact is that without it none would have become a true champion.

The quality I'm talking about is summarised best in a speech that Sir Winston Churchill once gave to a graduation class when he said, 'I have but ten words to say to you . . . no matter what happens never, ever, ever, ever give up.'

Each of our champions could have given the same speech!

Printed in the United States
By Bookmasters